PAINT
THE TOWN
BLACK

PAINT THE TOWN BLACK

Arthur Black

HARBOUR PUBLISHING

Harbour Publishing Co. Ltd.
PO Box 219, Madeira Park, BC, V0N 2H0
www.harbourpublishing.com

Edited by Margaret Tessman
Text design Mary White
Cover photo by Howard Fry
Cover design by Anna Comfort O'Keeffe
Printed and bound in Canada

Harbour Publishing acknowledges the support of the Canada
Council for the Arts, which last year invested $157 million to
bring the arts to Canadians throughout the country. We also grate-
fully acknowledge financial support from the Government of
Canada through the Canada Book Fund and from the Province
of British Columbia through the BC Arts Council and the Book
Publishing Tax Credit.

 Canada Council   Conseil des Arts
for the Arts   du Canada

 BRITISH COLUMBIA
ARTS COUNCIL
An agency of the Province of British Columbia

Cataloguing data available from Library and Archives Canada
    ISBN 978-1-55017-701-5 (paper)
    ISBN 978-1-55017-702-2 (ebook)

Contents

Part 1

SALT SPRING, MON AMOUR

Yes, We Have Some Bananas

I want to tell you about Banana Joe. No, not Joe Bananas. Different guy. Joe Bananas was the nickname for Giuseppe Bonanno, a Sicilian import who ran the New York Mafia back in the last century. I'm talking about Banana Joe, a guy who lives in the here and now on Salt Spring Island. You may have spotted him on the ferry, slouched next to his big black Harley. Joe in his wrap-around shades, decked out in black leather from chinstrap to boot heel. He's tattooed, got a wicked-looking goatee. He's tall, lean, kind of fierce-looking. That's Banana Joe.

Don't be fooled. Man's a pussycat.

Banana Joe's only a part-time biker. Full time he's a gardener here on Salt Spring. Why "Banana" Joe? Because the man is bananas. He's bananas for well, banana plants, windmill palms, Tasmanian tree ferns, flowering ginger—pretty much any plant that has no business whatsoever appearing in the same sentence as the words "Canadian winter"—even Canadian winters as mild as the ones you find in the Gulf Islands.

Most botanists would tell you that such plants are tropical, that there's no way they could survive any Canadian winter. Joe grows them all anyway, here on Salt Spring. Walk onto his property on the north end of the island and you expect Rossano Brazzi to start ululating "Some Enchanted Evening." You feel like you've stumbled onto the movie set for a remake of *South Pacific*.

But it's not just Banana Joe's place that's been Bali Hai'ed. Because he's been around for a few decades, Joe's spread his seed, as it were. Truth is, palm trees and banana trees aren't all that uncommon on the island, thanks to Joe. How many are there? Enough to fill a book. Joe's just put out a limited edition coffee table hardcover called *Subtropical Flora and Gardens*. The plants within those pages all live and thrive right here on Salt Spring.

So pervasive is Joe's influence that even I—whose name, Arthur Black Thumb, is muttered in whispers among gardening circles—even I have a windmill palm in my front yard.

And yes, a banana tree.

It doesn't look much like a banana tree right now. It looks like a wino in a burlap overcoat but pretty soon, as the ground warms up and as per Joe's instructions, my banana tree will shed its dingy winter garb, turn vibrant green and shoot up, up, up through the summer months to produce bananas in the fall.

Okay, they won't look much like bananas. They'll look like a cluster of wrinkled cigarillos and even the crows won't eat them, but what do you expect? I live on a Canadian island, not a Chiquita plantation in Nicaragua. I spent much of my adult life in northwestern Ontario where growing tomatoes that turned red qualified you for the Johnny Appleseed Hall of Fame. I'm not going to quibble about a few under-performing bananas.

Here on Salt Spring? I'll settle for tiny wizened bananas that look like Hugh Hefner's worst nightmare. I'm happy to see any bananas in my garden. And I happily tip my hat to Banana Joe for making it possible.

Apple Abundance

*I*f there was ever any doubt that words are living things, capable of growing and changing as dramatically as a geranium or a golden retriever puppy, consider the word apple.

When I was a kid everybody knew what an apple was—a juicy handful of nutrition that smelled like heaven, tasted divine and quite literally grew on trees. Then suddenly Apple became a British record company pumping out LPs for a group that called themselves The Beatles. And finally not so many years ago Apple became a Silicon Valley corporation producing laptops and cellphones and tablets. Perhaps its most famous product— the Mac—was even named after Steve Jobs' favourite variety of apple—the McIntosh.

Even though he spelled it wrong. The fruit McIntosh is a Mc, not a Mac.

Details, details. On Salt Spring I am pleased to announce that the apple for the most part is still a fleshy fruit that grows on trees. Has been since the 1800s when European settlers planted carefully hoarded apple seeds they'd saved from fruit they munched on the long voyage to Canada. One of those pioneers, Samuel Beddis, eventually planted 4,600 seedlings back in 1855 right around my neighbourhood. This morning I stepped out and plucked a Gravenstein off a gnarly, snaggly old descendant of that man's work, which stands in my front yard.

There are still thousands of fruit-producing descendants of those old pioneers on this and other Gulf Islands. At one time Victoria was the epicentre of apple production in British Columbia and the Gulf Islands were the backbone of the apple production that made it possible.

Those were the years before irrigation and refrigeration when the Okanagan was just a dusty old hinterland. It's been a long time since apples paid the bills and backstopped this island's economy, but we haven't forgotten our debt. We have an Apple Festival every fall. It features a tour of apple farms, a chance to see some of the 350 different varieties we grow here and to taste over a hundred—that's right, a hundred—different varieties, on Harry Burton's farm alone. There is also the opportunity to take home the fragrant fruits of Salt Spring's famous Pie Ladies. Sorry, Gloria Steinem, but that's what they call themselves, with a fierce pride. And one bite of their product is guaranteed to stifle all gripers.

There are 16 farms, all open to the public, and local chefs throw some incredible lunches together for visitors. If you ever wanted to visit, or re-visit, Salt Spring, late September would be a good time to do it.

Come and taste some apples that you'll never find at Safeway or Thrifty Foods. Apples with names like Belle de Boskoop, Pink Pearl, Winekist, Duchess of Oldenburg, Blenheim Orange and Winter Banana, Ginger Gold and Grenadine.

Somehow through standardization and mass production, we've lost sight of how wonderful and various the so-called "simple" apple can be.

Well, not everyone's forgotten. Are you looking for something sweet? Tart? Gingery? Pearish? Lemony? Delicate? Hearty? Green/red/yellow? Small as a cherry, big as a grapefruit, long and skinny, short and plump?

As the folks who run the Salt Spring Apple Festival like to say, with just a wink toward Steve Jobs: There's an apple for that.

Salt Spring: AKA Beater Island

*P*eople often ask me, Art, they say, what about it? Is Salt Spring Island the Cuba of Canada? And I always reply, "Si, señor." There are indeed many similarities. We are both islands in the sea, situated off the coast of North America. We are both steeped in, or at least splashed with, Spanish culture. Cubans speak Spanish, while Salt Springers look out to islands with Spanish names like Galiano, Gabriola, Cortes, Valdez . . .

Indeed one of our neighbours, Quadra, is named after a Spanish navigator, Juan Francisco de la Bodega y Quadra. And speaking of neighbours, we both tiptoe warily around the same one. A large, noisy, belligerent and unpredictable guy who plays with guns.

After that the comparison sort of tails off. Cuba has sharks, Salt Spring has ling cod; Cuba has sugar cane, Salt Spring has stinging nettle; Cuba has 100 proof rum, Salt Spring has two-fours of Lucky Lager.

But there is one other thing we both share to a marked degree. Guaranteed if you are in downtown Havana or cruising through Ganges, you are going to see more beaters than you ever saw in your life. Beaters: sedans, half-tons and pickup trucks that are two, three, even four decades past their best-before date.

Now in Cuba old cars rule because of the American embargo. Cubans haven't been able to buy new American cars since the middle of the last century. That's why the sight of a '57 Chevy Impala festooned with welding marks or a '58 Galaxy wearing a coat of orange house paint are by no means unusual sightings on the streets of Cuba.

As for Salt Spring, most of the ancient vehicles you see on this island are entirely the fault of Richard Murakami. Richard runs the most famous auto repair shop on Salt Spring. Richard can fix pretty much anything but he specializes in what we call "Island Girls," old and decrepit—sometimes unbelievably decrepit—sedans and half-tons that anywhere else would have gone to the scrap yards decades ago. Richard is the patron saint of sickly Chevys, faulty Fords, doddery Datsuns, vitiated Volkswagens and palpitating Pontiacs. He is the Francis of Assisi for internal combustion engine vehicles on their deathbed.

Why does he do it? Because Richard's a big softie. Single moms with a limited income, young guys waiting for their first paycheque beseech him. Can he fix their radiator, heat pump, rear axle, windshield wiper, alternator for, you know, not too much money? He probably can and will.

If Richard had a yen for politics he could run for mayor of Salt Spring and win in a landslide. Never happen, though. Richard's got his hands full fixing beaters.

Richard's Japanese Canadian but whenever I think of him a Spanish word pops up.

Corazón. It's Spanish for "heart."

Richard Murakami's is *muy grande*.

Have a Nice Fright

I live on a rock surrounded by deep water, which is a windy way of saying I don't get out much. So it's a pretty big deal when a book tour sucks me into the belly of a WestJet 737 and flings me all the way to Ontario to flog my latest collection (*Fifty Shades of Black*, Douglas & McIntyre, $29.95, great stocking stuffer, end of commercial).

A trip from the West Coast boonies to the Canadian heartland gives a country bumpkin an opportunity to make some observations as to what the rest of the world is up to. First observation: What's with all the hand gizmos—the cellphones, the BlackBerrys, the iPhones? Oh, we have them on Salt Spring, too, but they're occasional accessories on the island, not a 24/7 lifeline. People on the island don't look like they're surgically attached to their gadgets, the way they do in Ontario. Walking through an airport, riding on the subway, sitting in a downtown restaurant is surreal, like hanging out with a gang of cyborgs. Nobody glances up or whistles a tune or looks out the windows or chats. They're all staring into their palms. Except when they're twiddling their thumbs and staring into their palms.

One plus about flying: it's the one time everybody's not riveted to their gizmos. Not allowed. But that, I read, may soon change.

Forces are afoot to convince the US Federal Communications Commission to allow cellphone use during flight.

I have only one response to the FCC proposal: Are you nuts? Who wants to listen to a roofing contractor order galvanized chimney flashing from his Indianapolis supplier at 35,000 feet? Or a caterwauling, "Hi honey I'm on my way should I pick up Chinese at the mall" call? Who wants to overhear ANY cell conversation in an airplane? Not the flight attendants; they're already distracted. Certainly not the other passengers; travel by air is unpleasant enough. The answer is the phone companies, which could jack up the rates for inflight calls, and the airlines, which would get a rake-off from those increased fees.

Do I sound peevish? I am peevish. I am writing these words on my laptop in seat 16F of WestJet flight 227 and I'm trying to look on the bright side. Yes, the food is mediocre and overpriced but on the bright side, my keyboard is cutting off circulation to my gut so I'm not very hungry. Yes, those flight attendant "do-do" announcements are repetitive and annoying ("We DO ask and DO require that you DO keep that seat belt fastened") but on the bright side, it's familiar, like an old dog smell. Yes, the guy beside me is snoring but on the bright side, at least he isn't drooling.

Strike that—he IS drooling.

My legs are asleep, I've been outduelled for the armrest and my bum is numb but on the bright side, we are descending over the Coast Mountains preparing to land in Vancouver. Pretty soon I'll be on a seaplane for the 20-minute hop to Salt Spring. The seaplane—a Beaver—is everything this Boeing 737 600 series is not. It's roomy, friendly—and way too noisy for anybody to use a cellphone.

Salt Spring: The Cellphone Graveyard

You know what I think is the very best thing about living on Salt Spring? Cellphone reception. It's terrible on the island. Well, on big chunks of the island anyway. A lot of first-time visitors arriving by ferry at the south end are mystified by what I call the Fulford Harbour Phenomenon. It's not uncommon at the ferry dock in Fulford Harbour to see some citizens whirling around in circles holding their hands to their heads as if they've got intense headaches. They aren't members of some bizarre Sufi cult and they're not in pain. They are real estate agents who've suddenly lost their cell connection to a client. If you get close enough you'll hear their telltale plaintive cry: "CAN'T HEAR YOU, YOU'RE BREAKING UP! CAN'T HEAR YOU, YOU'RE BREAKING UP!"

Much of Salt Spring Island is enveloped in a black hole or, as I prefer to think of it, a Cathedral of Quiet, which deflects wireless transmissions and renders most cellphones utterly useless or at least unreliable.

This blessed cell-free zone disappears just a few hundred yards off shore, so if you're on a BC Ferry coming to or leaving the island, reception is just fine. Which means you can be sure your ferry nap will be interrupted by a one-sided conversation that will go something like this:

"HI, HONEY. IT'S ME, FRED." Everybody in the lounge, whether they're reading or relaxing or just trying to nap, glares at Fred. He doesn't notice. "YEAH. JUST COMING IN TO TSAWWASSEN NOW. YEAH, I KNOW I WAS SUPPOSED TO BE ON THE THREE THIRTY BUT I WORKED LATE. NO, I DIDN'T GO TO THE OFFICE PARTY. I AM NOT SLURRING. I AM NOT CALLING FROM SOME MOTEL LOBBY! I'M ON THE SPIRIT OF BRITISH COLUMBIA FERRY! OF COURSE I LOVE YOU. OF COURSE THERE'S NO ONE ELSE."

Personally I've never known what to do about guys like Fred on their cellphones. My crocodile brain says to grab him by his tie and the seat of his pants and throw him into the Salish Sea but that would mean complications. And possibly jail time. I've considered telling Fred to shut the hell up but sometimes Fred is larger and younger than me and that would mean complications. And possibly hospital time.

I like the way the lady who was sitting right next to Fred handled it. Fred was just explaining over the phone that, "BABY BELIEVE ME THERE'S NO ONE ELSE. YOU'RE MY ITTY BITTY SNUGGLE BUNNY BABY," when the lady sitting next to him leaned over toward Fred and his cellphone and said in her sexiest voice, "Come on Fred, stop talking on the phone and come back to bed."

Sure hope Fred's reception died before Snuggle Bunny heard that.

Dodgy Island Characters

The place I call home is about 150 million years old. Actually, it's even older than that, but 150 million years ago is when a massive shelf of rock bumped into the west coast of what would one day be North America, buckled and heaved and eventually settled down to form Vancouver Island, Alaska, Haida Gwaii and 200 or so stony little dots and dashes that would one day be called the Gulf Islands. In the ensuing millennia glaciers would come and go, sculpting and fine-tuning those dots and dashes. Then about 12,000 years ago, give or take a long weekend, some two-legged mammals appeared, liked what they saw and stayed.

Which begs the question, what is it about the Gulf Islands that attracts settlers? What is it that's different, that keeps drawing those two-legged mammals 12,000 years later?

Well, a lot of things. Just living on an island will make you different. You've got several miles of unpredictable salt water separating you from your neighbours. There's no Walmart, or Cineplex or airport on the edge of town. And the experience even varies from island to island. Living on Lasqueti is different from living on Pender is different from living on Gabriola. I can't speak for those islands but I can speak for Salt Spring and I'll tell you one thing that makes my island quite different from any place I've ever lived before.

Draft dodgers.

We've got a lot of American draft dodgers woven into the warp and weft of the Salt Spring tapestry. Tens of thousands of Americans left the US during the Vietnam War alone. Most of them came to Canada and a lot of those washed up on Salt Spring. In the country they left they were pariahs, subject to persecution and prosecution. But in Canada they were just immigrants. We didn't ask them about their draft status or keep records once they landed. An awful lot of them stayed and went on to become Canadian architects, lawyers, musicians, writers, professors, teachers.

As a country we've done this before. Back during the American Revolution there was another influx of Americans dissatisfied with the direction their country was headed. They came north. We called them United Empire Loyalists. Many of them also became pillars of Canadian society, from farmers and ranchers to scholars and businessmen.

It's an interesting form of one-way cross-border commerce. Canada doesn't receive many John Waynes or Rush Limbaughs or foaming-at-the-mouth, live-free-or-die patriots in the transaction. Those types tend to stay south of the border. We get the quiet ones, the doubters, the, well, more Canadian types. It's not totally cut and dried of course. We did have Ted Cruz for a bit. He was born in Calgary but we shipped him south COD as soon as we could.

Salt Spring's draft dodgers are old-timers now. Like the island they live on, they've been sculpted and sanded down over the years. Their accents have eroded. They say out and about instead of owt and abowt. They follow Canucks hockey, for better or worse. They're Salt Springers. And they're Canadians. Beauty deal, eh?

Emu, Brutus?

Sometimes when I'm at the Salt Spring market in downtown Ganges a tourist will ask me how to get to Beddis Beach. Easy, I tell them, just go up the hill and turn left on Beddis Road, keep going past the yak farm on the right and the miniature ponies on the left, watch out for the Jersey cows and be careful not to hit the free-range peacocks and keep going till you see the Beddis Beach sign. If you get to a flock of emus you've gone too far.

Yeah, we have emus on Salt Spring. Not wild like the peacocks and the deer. These emus are caged. But you never know, do you? Look at that emu desperado Lucy, up Nanaimo way. Lucy was behind wire but managed to bust out and lead Nanaimo police, fire, and search and rescue workers a merry chase until he was finally cornered after five days on the lam. Yes, I said he. Lucy is a guy. Hey, could YOU tell a guy emu from a girl emu? Well, neither could Lucy's owner until the vet filled him in.

Frankly I'm surprised anybody ever got a lasso on Lucy. We are talking about a bird that stands six feet high, weighs as much as a middleweight boxer and has a cruising speed of 60 klicks an hour. That's running, you understand. The emu is covered with feathers but it can't fly. The wings are puny. Vestigial. That's why, with the rest of Nanaimo in lockdown, during the search for Lucy authorities didn't even bother to monitor the airport.

They knew Lucy was on the No Fly list.

In any case when it comes to flight or fight, emus don't need to fly. They can kick. Those long muscular legs end in three size-13 leathery toes, each capped by a talon the length of your baby finger. Not only can the emu kick, it can disembowel. Which is why most predators give emus a wide berth.

They're pretty curious about humans, though, and they're shameless moochers. Which is why the Beddis Road emu enclosure boasts a big sign that reads PLEASE DON'T FEED THE EMUS. If visitors fed the emus they'd look like butterballs in no time.

Come to think of it, they do look like butterballs. Large, feathery, 150-pound butterballs.

Visitors are welcome to look, though. Even take pictures if you like. If you're lucky the birds will line up along the fence for you. They are photogenic as all get out. There's Emil. And Emily. And Emma. And Emmanuelle. Which one is which? Hey, they're emus. Your guess is as good as mine.

Don't worry about it. Enjoy yourself. Take a selfie with a slice of Salt Spring's wildest wildlife.

Just don't make any off-the-cuff remarks about drumsticks.

Having a Gay Old Time

I knew it was going to be an unusual day when I went to pay for my newspaper at Salt Spring Books. Kelly, the lady behind the counter, was wearing a fluorescent chartreuse dress, a pink chiffon scarf and three scarlet rhododendrons around her left ear.

That's unusual. Even for Salt Spring.

Or maybe not. Not on Parade Day at least.

That would be the annual Pride Parade day held last September on Salt Spring. They call it the Gay Pride parade but that's hardly accurate. It's really the Gay Straight Lesbian Bi Transsexual Transgender Intersex and Questioning Pride Parade. And everybody was in it. There was a Nanaimo Pride contingent and a delegation from the Queer Bawdies burlesque troupe in Vancouver. I spotted a bunch from the Salt Spring United Church and a party from the island Buddhist meditation group. The Salt Spring Japanese Garden Society entered a tractor that carried seven people, three dogs and two chickens. There were Unitarians, firefighters, schoolteachers, librarians, search and rescue technicians—even a lone participant in an orange wig, a mini skirt, a bustier . . . and a Vandyke goatee. My personal favourite: a float sponsored by the BC Ferry and Marine Workers Union that featured two broad-shouldered employees in frocks, five-o'clock shadows and high heels, one of whom announced to the crowds, "Folks, you're looking at a fairy who can out-pull any BC ferry, lemme tell ya."

The parade pretty well closed the town for two hours on Saturday—well, to vehicle traffic, anyway. The joint was jumping with camped-up pedestrians ranging from Green Party leader Elizabeth May to my favourite cashier at Country Grocer. There was even an Academy Award winner. Jim Erickson, the Salt Springer who won for Best Set Design on the movie *Lincoln*, was in a vintage car cradling his shiny Oscar on his lap. "Hold it up!" I yelled from the sidelines. "C'mere!" he replied. I walked over to the car and he thrust the statuette into my hands. "You try holding it up," he said.

Caramba! Who knew that an Oscar weighs eight and a half pounds?

It was a grand parade with drummers and clowns and at times it felt like the whole town was boogying to a salsa beat.

A bit confusing at times, though. I mean . . . guys dancing with guys, girls dancing with girls. Guys dancing with girls dancing with kids dancing with grandmas. There's my pal George who I shoot pool with. George is 83 years old. He's about as gay as Don Cherry. And he's wearing a floor-length rainbow cape.

Why, sometimes you couldn't tell who was gay and who was straight.

Which of course was the entire point of the exercise. Gay Straight Lesbian Bi Transsexual Transgender Intersex or Questioning.

What's it matter?

Salt Spring's Sacred Geyser

*I*f you want to experience the ineffable bliss of life on a Gulf Island (and who this side of Stephen Harper doesn't?) there are worse atolls to pick than my own, Salt Spring. What's to see? Scenery, for starters. Some say the island is nothing but scenery—from Ruckle Park in the south end to Southey Point in the, er, north end. Lots more than that—art galleries, restaurants, live music venues, funky shopping at the Saturday market, black helicopters looking for the mythical grow ops . . .

And one other thing.

We have the Sacred Geyser. Sure. France has the spring at Lourdes, England has the Chalice Well at Glastonbury, Florida's got the Fountain of Youth in St. Augustine, India has the sacred Ganges River, Salt Spring's got . . . well, the Ganges Geyser. Actually it's more of a seep or leak but those aren't words you'd use in a tourism ad. Never mind. What it lacks in spectacularity it more than makes up for in location.

The Ganges Geyser is indecently handy. It's in the only town we've got—Ganges. In downtown Ganges. In fact, it's right in the middle of the main street of downtown Ganges.

It first appeared, mysteriously, miraculously, a couple of years ago when the burghers of Ganges woke up to find water running down the middle of the Fulford–Ganges road. Not an unheard of experience here in the middle of the rainforest, except that it wasn't raining. Hadn't rained for several days. For the next few weeks the Ganges Geyser continued to . . . geyse. Eventually (and we're talking Island Time here, so it was a long eventually, but eventually) a works crew showed up, dug a little, leaned on their shovels a little more and concluded that a drain was needed. Two six-inch perforated pipes were installed and directed into a nearby creek. The works crew filled the hole, patched the road and went away. Problem solved.

Not.

A year after the road was closed and patched the Ganges Geyser is back, stronger than ever. In fact a small dip in the road has appeared—evidence, some alarmists say, of an underground cavity that's probably beginning to form.

I say nonsense. And don't call it a cavity. That's so . . . orthodontic.

You know the old cliché about when life hands you lemons, make lemonade? Well, we need to make some Salish Sea lemonade here. So don't call it a cavity for starters. Call it a grotto.

Sure! Lourdes has a sacred grotto; St. Augustine's got a photo-op grotto. We need a grotto to go with the geyser. We could call it the Blessed Sanctuary of St. Valdimir—Valdy, for short. Sell postcards. T-shirts. Lucky St. Valdy necklaces made of authentic certified and urethaned Salt Spring deer poop strung on braided hemp.

It's a natural, I tell ya. All we have to do is install a turnstile and start printing tickets.

And holy water? Holy Hannah! Pilgrims travel from all over the world to Lourdes to get vials of holy water but thanks to airport security they can no longer take them on airplanes when they go home. Well, that's no problem when you leave Salt Spring. BC Ferries doesn't care how much water you bring aboard. They're used to water.

So make your next vacation a Salt Spring odyssey. Come visit the Ganges Geyser and fill a vial. Fill a bucket. Fill your boots.

Just Itching to Garden

A garden is always a series of losses set against a few triumphs, like life itself.

MAY SARTON

*J*ohnny Charlton bloodied my nose in the cloakroom in Grade 5.

Judy Houston broke my heart behind the school bleachers in Grade 9.

The Toronto Maple Leafs have caused me to hurl popcorn and verbal abuse at my TV screen every spring since Lester Pearson was prime minister.

I have known Grief and Loss.

But I know of no source of pain and disappointment so consistent and capricious as that backyard rectangle of botanical bushwhackery: my vegetable garden.

Actually the very adjective "vegetable" is a cruel jest akin to a slap in the face with a wet rhubarb leaf. My garden produces vegetables as a distant afterthought. Primarily it manufactures blisters, perspiration, heartbreak and underarm rash. It also functions as a nursery for moles, voles, mice, rabbits and, last year, a ground nest of decidedly grumpy and territorial yellow jackets.

It's not as if I'm a gardening greenhorn. I've read the how-to books. I've signed up for and followed the online gardening courses. Lord knows I've bought the tools. I've got enough rakes, forks, hoes, spades, trowels, pruners, clippers and trimmers in my garden shed to open my own Lee Valley franchise. The only garden tool I haven't bought (and desperately need) is a well-oiled stainless steel hinge. For my back.

And it's not as if I live in Death Valley or Pangnirtung. I live on the bucolic shores of the West Coast Canadian rainforest, which is to say a land of fertile soil, abundant rain and more than adequate sunshine. I'm surrounded by ridiculously fecund farmland that regularly pumps out bumper crops of fruits and vegetables worthy of ribbons at the fall fair. Not me and not mine. I've tried for years and failed. Every spring I plant tomatoes, kale, carrots, potatoes and corn. Every fall I harvest chickweed, twitch grass, plantain, purslaine, lamb's quarters, pigweed, horsetails and yellow toad-flax. Not to mention a particularly tenacious local intruder known as creeping charlie. I know. It sounds like an infiltrating Viet Cong death squad. Ironic, that.

Chicken manure. That's what my pal Martin said I needed. He'd been growing his own food for half a century in these parts and he said what I needed was chicken manure.

Actually, the term he used was earthier and I'm still not sure whether he was talking about the garden or the gardener, but never mind. I got myself some chicken manure. Found a farmer with an abandoned chicken coop and bought a pickup truckload of the stuff. Dumped the whole load, deep and crisp and even, over my garden. Worked it into my soil with my own bare hands kneading and caressing every tiny lump of . . .

Never mind. There's such a thing as too much information.

"Whaddya think?" I murmured to my Life Companion, one arm around her shoulders, the other scratching absently.

"Chicken manure," she mumbled. Actually, she too used the earthier version, also without specific attribution.

She too was scratching absently.

"You itchy?" I asked. Turns out she was. We both were.

Mites. From the chicken manure. Tens, possibly hundreds of thousands of the wriggly little buggers. And they liked our house even more than they liked the garden.

The fumigation was only slightly more expensive than the

motel (we had to find one willing to take us, two dogs, a cat and a cockatoo) but it worked out okay in the end. And Martin was right—that chicken manure worked wonders. We harvested cobs of corn as big as your forearm. Cabbages the size of basketballs. And tomatoes? We brought in groaning wheelbarrow loads of succulent, bulging tomatoes worthy of Findhorn. Would you like one? I can let you have it at cost. Pick yourself a nice fat juicy one.

That'll be $37.75. Plus GST.

Busting Out on Salt Spring

*P*eople think that because Salt Spring is an island full of rheu-matic retirees and superannuated hippies we are somehow removed from the grittier problems that plague bigger cities and towns. Don't be fooled. Salt Spring has its share of big time crime, buster. Like the daring midnight jailbreak that went down a couple of weekends ago.

Didn't hear about that, did you? No. Nothing on *The National.* Not an inch of ink in the *Vancouver Sun* or *Province.* My theory: Salt Spring Chamber of Commerce probably paid big bucks to put a lid on it.

Well, now it can be told. The escape artists? I'll name names. A hardened felon named Maggie Monsanto, well known, as they say, to authorities, and her sidekick, Farley. Let's be clear from the start: Maggie M. is the alpha con in this breakout caper. Farley has always been a bit of an ass.

Actually, Farley is an ass. A full-blooded ass. You know, a donkey. And Maggie Monsanto—she's a mule. No, not a drug mule, a mule mule. The offspring of a horse and a donkey. She got the surname Monsanto because, well, like many of Monsanto's more unnatural products, she's a sterile hybrid. All mules are.

Anyway, point of the story: Friday, October 13, 2013, 10:45

p.m. Maggie and Farley are doing time at the animal exhibit at the Salt Spring Fall Fair grounds. Maggie gets a brainwave. She says to Farley in fluent Mulese: "We oughtta blow this pop stand."

"How?" brays Farley. "Leave it to me," says Maggie.

She's found a rotten fencepost. She applies her ample bum and leans. Craaaaaaaaaaaaaaaaaack. The fence goes down. They've busted out.

As jailbreaks go it was doomed from the start. Salt Spring ain't Alcatraz but it is an island. And even a street-savvy mule accompanied by a furtive four-footed sidekick is going to have trouble flagging down a ride or clip-clopping onto a BC Ferry undetected. Maggie and Farley eluded authorities until the wee hours of Saturday morning but eventually, posses heavily armed with carrots and pails of warm bran tracked them down, collared them and led them back to their cell, er, corral.

Caroline Hickman, who as owner is head warden over Maggie and Farley, scoffs when people try to tell her that Maggie and Farley were "just lost" and "trying to find their way home." "That's a Disney fantasy," says Hickman. She has no illusions about the hard-bitten criminals in her care. "Those two were out to have a party night in Ganges, a wild Friday night," she says.

And the fact that this Friday happened to be a Friday the 13th?

Coincidence. Crime isn't based on astrology and it's an unlucky day when criminals strike no matter what the calendar says. And it doesn't just happen in big city tenderloins and shady metropolitan back alleys. It can happen anywhere. Even on Salt Spring. Oh, it looks bucolic and peaceful out there but don't be fooled. This place is a zoo.

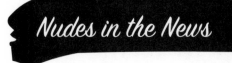

Nudes in the News

I see that Judy Williams is in the news again. Judy is chief spokes-person for the WBPS and as such she's, well, not ticked off exactly. She's way too diplomatic for that. She's concerned, shall we say, that the Mounties are planning to patrol her turf. WBPS stands for Wreck Beach Preservation Society and that is Judy's turf. She is a nudist and a champion for Vancouver's defiantly nude outdoor venue. The society has been protecting and patrolling their sandy turf since 1983.

The local Mountie detachment is concerned about public safety on Wreck Beach, so much so that Sgt. Drew Grainger says members of his unit will be pitching a tent on the beach each summer weekend through until Labour Day. Judy says, "Not necessary." The skinheads (and skin everything else) of Wreck Beach have been patrolling themselves for as long as anyone can remember. "We're an extended family," says Judy. "The beach people don't want a police presence. We have a good relationship with the police but we disagree on this."

That sounds just like Judy—fair but firm. I have a . . . slight history with the woman. As a matter of fact on my office wall there's a framed picture of Judy and I sitting on a log on Wreck Beach about 15 years ago doing an interview for my radio show.

In the photo I'm wearing a baseball cap and a microphone; Judy is wearing . . . less.

I'm not a practising nudist myself, but I have no problem with it—kinda in favour of it, as a matter of fact. Besides, I can see no end of problems for the cops on this one. For starters, just how "undercover" are the Wreck Beach Mountie patrols prepared to get? Will they wear gun belts? Can they keep their Smokey the Bear hats on? What are they going to pin their badges to?

It's urban conundrums like this that make me doubly glad to live on Planet Salt Spring. We don't have a nudist beach problem on the island because we don't have a nudist beach.

We have a nudist lake.

It's called Blackburn Lake, more of a big pond really, located near the belly of the island just off the highway and down a leafy laneway right next to a wildlife sanctuary.

And unlike at Wreck Beach you don't have to worry about being buzzed by drunken boater yokels. No boats. Blackburn is landlocked.

Our Chamber of Commerce won't tell you that Blackburn is for nudists. If pressed, they might allow that it's "clothing optional." And while it's true that you don't absolutely have to be starkers to swim at Blackburn, you'll stand out like a sore thumb if you're not.

Speaking of sore, I'm doubly glad that Salt Spring's nudist waterhole is Blackburn Lake, not Wreck Beach. Our lake is close to civilization. If you started taking off your clothes at the entrance, you wouldn't even be down to your socks by the time you hit the water. Wreck Beach? There's a 465-step staircase you have to go up to get back to Marine Drive after you've spent the day lying on a beach blanket.

Try that when you've got sunburnt in places you never had sunburn before.

TWO STEPS FORWARD, THREE STEPS BACK

Sign Here, Please

Peter Gzowski, the late CBC radio star, had the smallest one I've ever seen—looked like an inchworm with hiccups. John Hancock's, on the other hand, was colossal. And magnificent. He laid it right across the bottom of the parchment of the American Declaration of Independence and declared, "There. I guess King George will be able to see that."

Calm yourself, madame—it's signatures we're talking about here. Signatures are an ancient and rather old-fashioned method of personal identification. We use our signatures to validate our drivers' licences, personal cheques, leases, wedding vows, speeding tickets, petitions, hotel registries . . . the list goes on.

The irony is, our signatures are often unreadable. Gzowski's, as I mentioned, was a nondescript squiggle, unrelated, as far as I could see, to any letter in the alphabet. Mine isn't much better—a touch more flamboyant but illegible to the uninitiated.

But much, much better than Jack Lew's. Mr. Lew is the US Secretary of the Treasury and his signature has made him the butt of jokes on late-night TV shows.

It's just a series of joined circles—seven or eight of them. It looks like the famous Olympics logo run amok. President Obama said (with a wink) that he'd had second thoughts about the appointment, seeing that the secretary's signature will appear on US currency. Jack Lew has promised to "work on it."

Maybe he won't have to. It seems that signatures are passé.

In fact, it seems that handwriting is almost passé too. A recent British survey shows that one in every three children struggles with cursive writing and one in five slips into "texting" language when they do put pen or pencil to paper.

And they can't depend on guidance from their parents. Twenty percent of the parents contacted in the same survey admitted they hadn't written a single letter by hand in the past year.

We can't expect much help from the educational system either. Down in the US, the National Governors Association has decreed new standards for the school curriculum and it's all about computers. The association calls for proficiency in keyboarding by Grade 4. What are they going to drop to achieve that? Elementary, my dear Watson—handwriting. Right now, American kids receive 15 minutes of handwriting instruction per day. That's down from 30 to 45 minutes for the previous generation. Next stop: zero.

Supporters say, about time. They point out that retina scans and computer fingerprinting are already replacing signatures, so who needs signatures?

And my signature? It's still illegible but that doesn't mean it's not important. The other day I was signing a receipt for a credit card purchase when the clerk pointed out that the signature slot on my card was blank. I'd forgotten to sign it.

"I'm afraid I can't let you buy this, sir," said the clerk.

I asked why. Because, he said, the signature on my receipt had to match the signature on the card.

I took the card and signed it. The clerk took it back and carefully compared it to the signature on the receipt.

Lucky for me they matched.

Use Your Head

*W*ant to get in on the very latest nightlife trend? Here's what to do: first find a good book, preferably a thick one, and then wait for my call. One evening soon you will receive instructions to take your book and proceed to a well-appointed club room well off the main drag. When you arrive you will be directed to an easy chair with good lighting. Don't look for waiters. There is no food or beverage service. There is no talking. Most especially there is no access to social media. For the next three hours you and the people around you will not text; neither will you tweet, check your email or play Angry Birds.

You will simply read your books.

After three hours the embargo is lifted. Participants are free to interact the old-fashioned way—eye contact, smiles, a hand on the forearm, words coming out of the mouth, that sort of thing. These Silent Reading Parties are springing up all over. According to a report in the *New Yorker* magazine, attendees appreciate being urged to get out of their homes to read, and they are grateful for the peer pressure that keeps them from covertly peeking at their iPhones and androids.

It's not easy. Of all the fallout from new social media one of the least examined is attention fragmentation. More and more we seem to fear being alone—even for seconds. Does this explain the suicidal insanity of texting while driving? The comedian Louis C.K. thinks so.

"Sometimes when things clear away and you're not watching anything and you're in your car and you start going, oh no, here it comes . . . it starts to visit on you, just this sadness. That's why we text and drive. People are willing to risk taking a life and ruining their own. They don't want to be alone for a second because it's so hard."

Louis is right. A team at the University of Virginia recently conducted an experiment on 700 people. The concept was simple: put individuals in a room by themselves with no access to tablets, cellphones, PCs or Macs. Leave them with only their brains for company. After a while bring them out and ask them how they feel.

Bad, it turns out. Very, very bad. A majority said they found it "very unpleasant" to be alone with their thoughts even for 15 minutes.

In one experiment, 64 percent of men and 15 percent of women began administering electric shocks to themselves (an option they'd been given, even though no one asked for it). Turned out a majority preferred physical pain to, you know, thinking.

It didn't matter if the experiments were conducted in the sterile confines of a laboratory or in the comfort of the participants' homes. It didn't help if the subjects were given topics to "think about" such as summer vacations, sports events or what they looked for in a partner. Timothy Wilson, the psychology professor who ran the experiments, concluded, "They just didn't like being in their own heads."

My mom, bless her, used to admonish her kids to "use your brains."

"Your brain is a muscle," she'd say. "If you don't use it, it shrivels away."

Mom's grasp of human physiology was sketchy but she had a point.

Now That's Television!

I don't know if this is a record but I haven't watched TV since 1985.

Regular programming, I mean. I continue to tune in if the weather looks particularly growly, there's an election going on or we still have a Canadian team in the Stanley Cup playoffs.

Or if I happen to find myself in some part of the country that carries the Log Fire Channel.

Are you familiar with the Log Fire Channel? I discovered it by accident years ago in Thunder Bay. Turned on a TV to the local Maclean-Hunter cable channel and there it was—a log fire burning in a fireplace in full, blazing colour. No voice-over, no commentary. No annoying used car hustlers or commercials for detergents, beer or banks; no blow-dried news readers keeping me abreast of the latest body count in the Middle East. Just a fire, burning peacefully in a fireplace.

I guess from time to time the logs were replenished by an unseen hand, but I can't say for sure. I was mesmerized by the simple beauty of a burning fire.

Norwegians know all about this. Each year NRK, the Norwegian public broadcaster, puts on a National Firewood Night—12 straight hours of a TV camera trained on a burning fireplace. Over 20 percent of Norwegian TV watchers tune in. CBC programmers would sacrifice their mothers for numbers like that.

The success of National Firewood Night emboldened NRK to try other broadcasting adventures. In 2009 viewers got to ride vicariously on the cowcatcher of the Bergensbanen, a train that chugs through tunnels and mountains and valleys and plains between Oslo and Bergen. More than a million Norwegians went along for the trip—on their TV sets.

This past winter viewers were treated to 18 hours of salmon swimming upstream. Anyone who found that plot too complicated could watch 100 hours of Norwegian grandmaster Magnus Carlsen pondering his next chess move.

Other epics on NRK: five straight days on a cruise ship plying the west coast of Norway; or a "sheep to sweater" docudrama that takes you from shearing the sheep through spinning the wool, through knit-one-purl-twoing the pattern all the way to finished product—a Norwegian sweater, natch.

It's slow TV—an idea whose time has come. Lise-May Spissey, the producer of the knitting marathon, encapsulates the concept perfectly. "All other TV is just speeding up," she told a German reporter. "We want to break with that. We want to allow people to finish their sentences."

Amen to that. And amen to the Log Fire Channel, wherever it burns. Life doesn't get much more beautiful or satisfying than the contemplation of a log fire burning in a fireplace. "Indian TV," Joseph Boyden called it in his wonderful book, *Through Black Spruce*. All I know is, I prefer it to most of the fare offered by the North American networks. If you're fortunate enough to get the Log Fire Channel, throw away your channel surfer. You don't need it.

Usonia the Beautiful

Canada could have enjoyed English government,
French culture and American know-how. Instead
it ended up with English know-how, French
government and American culture.

JOHN ROBERT COLOMBO

Yeah, well. We Canadians paid our dues for that imported American culture. James Cameron, the legendary film director? Canadian. Economist John Kenneth Galbraith? Canadian. Frank Gehry, the architect? Actor Lorne Greene? EugeneLevyMartinShortJohnCandyMikeMyersJimCarreyAvril-LavigneCelineDionNeilYoungPamelaAndersonShaniaTwain-JoniMitchell etc., etc.?

All famous, all Canadian. All traded to and living in America.

Not to mention Wayne Gretzky, Labatt's Blue and Molson (ahem) Canadian.

Damn Americans. They not only steal our talent and our beer, they steal our very name.

Why do they get to call themselves Americans? What about Mexicans? What about us? Yankees are just one layer of the North American sandwich. Other folks live here too. Such as, well, us.

This is not an original observation. The famous architect Frank Lloyd Wright thought his countrymen were behaving like rowdy house guests as far back as 1927. Even that wasn't original. Wright was quoting the idea of a nineteenth-century (ahem) American writer by the name of James Duff Law who wrote: "We of the United States, in justice to Canadians and Mexicans, have no right to use the title 'Americans' when referring to matters pertaining exclusively to ourselves." Mr. Law proposed the term "Usonia."

As in "A Usonian Werewolf in London" and "Bye, Bye Miss Usonian Pie."

Frank Lloyd went so far as to design what he called Usonian homes—houses specifically designed to be affordable to middle-income families. Wright oversaw the construction of about 60 Usonian houses throughout the US. They were made of native materials and recycled bricks, single-storey, flat-roofed, designed to take advantage of natural lighting and passive solar heating. This in the 1930s. Frank Lloyd Wright: a man just slightly ahead of his time.

Wright also rejected automobile garages in his Usonian houses. He considered them wasteful and unnecessary. In their place he designed an overhang with no walls that he called the "carport"—the first use of that term.

Alas, the Usonian house concept never caught on. Wright's potential clientele preferred big, sprawling and wasteful to compact and economical. More American, less Usonian.

Ah, well. Names are tricky and quixotic things. It's only by chance that our chunk of North America ended up being called Canada. Other names were on the table. Names like Laurentia, Cabotia, Ursania, Colonia.

And my favourite: Mesopelagia.

You think our national anthem is hard to sing? Try standing up at a hockey game and warbling, "Oooooh, Mesopelaaaaaagiaaaa . . . "

The Song Our Paddles Sing

I could carry, paddle, walk and sing with any man I ever saw . . . No portage was ever too long for me, fifty songs I could sing. I have had twelve wives and six running dogs. I spent all my money on pleasure. Were I young again, I would spend my life the same way over. There is no life so happy as a voyageur's life.

OLD VOYAGEUR, CIRCA 1825

I think "voyageur" is one of the most galvanic words in Canadian history. Imagine those guys! Fourteen-hour days squatting in birch bark shells, shoulders knotted, sweat popping off their brows, paddling a stroke a second, smashing through rapids, bogs and Great Lakes cloudbursts, sleeping under their canoes when the blackflies and mosquitoes allowed them to. And doing it from the top of the Lachine Rapids to the nethermost snout of Lake Superior.

And back. Every year between spring break-up and the autumn freeze. The voyageurs' exploits defined this country for nearly two centuries, and then faded from the scene as the beaver that drew them west grew sparse.

In the end they left no more mark than a paddle swirl on the water. And even less of a record, being mostly illiterate.

Voyageur. In English, "voyager": one who goes on a long and sometimes dangerous journey.

There is another voyager—called, in fact, Voyager 2. It is a NASA spacecraft in the thirty-sixth year of a profoundly perilous journey. It has travelled through our entire solar system, beyond Mars, Saturn, even Pluto.

Voyager 2 doesn't present anything close to the noble silhouette of a voyageur *canot du nord*. It looks like a collision of giant kitchen utensils, an ungainly mashup of antennae and probes attached to a dog's breakfast of scientific instruments. But it can fly. Voyager 2 has been moving away from Earth for nearly four decades now and is doubtless dented and scarred by its (so far) 16-billion mile voyage.

But get this. In the belly of Voyager 2 there is a golden disc. It is a recording of earth sounds destined for the ears of . . . well, who knows? Whoever or whatever is Out There. Any sentient being that can figure out how to access that disc will hear the sound of: A gust of wind, the patter of rain, human footsteps, the chitter of a chimpanzee, a baby's heartbeat, a mother's kiss and a burst of belly laughter.

Also, the music of Bach and Mozart. Plus Chuck Berry's "Johnny Be Good."

It was a galactic leap of faith. When Voyager 2 launched, the planet was knotted in a Cold War, famine and disease stalked huge swathes of Asia and Africa. A spectre called AIDS was just beginning to cast its shadow. The world, as it usually is, was a mess.

But out of the chaos, this: a cry to the universe that says: We're good. We can do beautiful things. We matter.

Carl Sagan, who helped choose the sound bites on the golden disc, said, "The launching of this bottle into the cosmic ocean says something very hopeful about life on this planet."

Indeed it does. It's a message any Canadian voyageur would understand in his bones.

It's All in Your Genes

A few years back George W. Bush, in between bankrupting his own country and laying waste to a couple of others, paused to make a dress code pronouncement. "There will be," thundered the 43rd president of the United States, "no blue jeans in the Oval Office."

If a backhanded endorsement like that didn't guarantee fashion immortality for a line of pants, nothing could.

That snorting sound? Just old Levi Strauss chortling in his grave.

Mr. Strauss is the man who started the whole blue jeans phenomenon. A century and a half ago, during the great gold rush, Strauss was just another San Francisco johnny-come-lately merchant trying to turn a buck by selling dry goods to gold seekers. He met a tailor who had come up with a way to use copper rivets to reinforce blue denim work pants. Strauss advanced him the $68 patent fee in return for half interest in the business. In 1873 a factory with "Levi Strauss & Company" hand painted on a wooden board over the entrance opened its doors. All it made was blue jeans.

Last year $16 billion worth of blue jeans were sold in the US alone.

And believe it or not, that's the bad news.

Jeans sales actually fell 6 percent last year, for the first time in decades. Not that they'll disappear anytime soon. Blue jeans still account for 20 percent of annual sales in US department stores.

Old Levi would have trouble seeing the connection with the product he sold to gold miners back in the 1870s. Levi's originals were no-nonsense and workmanlike, built for durability, not looks. And it was strictly one-style-fits-all. Today? If you've got the bucks you can choose from skinny, wide-leg, boot-cut, tapered, bell-bottom, drainpipe, low-rise or hip-hugger. Not to mention a few non-Levi's brands like Lee and Wrangler.

Modern blue jeans even have the Aging Boomer market covered. Has gravity had its way with you, leaving you with a pot-belly, bowed legs and a withered butt? Chill, bro—we've got you covered. You can still look trendy in "relaxed" or "stretch" jeans.

You can buy jeans that look like they just came out of the store, but it's not considered terribly cool. That's why many customers opt for jeans that come pre-ripped and factory-distressed. Jeans that make you look like you've been dragged behind a runaway stagecoach for a couple of miles.

Naturally you'll pay more for that. In fact if you're a real jeans fanatic it's not hard to drop $300 for a pair of state-of-the-art blue jeans.

That would have Levi rotating in his grave. That and this quote: "I wish I had invented blue jeans: the most spectacular, the most practical, the most relaxed and nonchalant. They have expression, modesty, sex appeal, simplicity—all I hope for in my clothes."

I didn't say that. Those are the words of fashion giant Yves Saint Laurent. Not only was he a giant in the fashion world, he was a man who looked good in skinny jeans. Yves knew the secret. You only need one thing to look good in skinny jeans:

Skinny genes.

Too Many Choices

Nothing is more difficult and therefore more precious than to be able to decide.

NAPOLEON BONAPARTE

*D*ecisions, decisions. If you ask me, Napoleon had it easy. Consider what would happen if the half-pint general found himself around today in, oh, say the local Safeway or Loblaws. Let's suppose he has a hankering for some breakfast cereal. Casting his eye over the supermarket offerings General B. would see:

Apple Cinnamon, Honey Nut, Multi Grain, Oats and Honey, Banana Nut, Multi Grain Peanut Butter, Cinnamon Burst, Chocolate, Frosted, Fruity and Regular.

And that would be just the Cheerios shelf.

Care for a Coke, General? You can choose from Classic, Lemon, Cherry, Vanilla, Black Cherry Vanilla, Citra, Raspberry or Coke Orange.

Not to mention Diet Coke, Coke Zero, Caffeine-free Coke, Coke C2, Coke Life and Coke Light. There's even MexiCoke—Coca-Cola that's imported from Mexico. It's made with cane sugar instead of the usual corn syrup and it's reputed to deliver an amplified "buzz."

And if the name Coca-Cola offends you, not to worry. The same company produces and sells Tab, Fanta and Sprite.

No matter what they call it it's all just flavoured water. And we spend billions of dollars a year guzzling the stuff.

Are we bored, too rich or just terminally gullible?

Maybe it's the latter. How else to explain that we now line up to pay for something that the earth gives us for free?

I'm talking about water. We not only line up to buy it, we buy it in plastic bottles that we then toss. Last year Americans discarded 35 billion plastic water bottles, only a fraction of which were recycled.

If you get your recommended daily eight glasses of water from plastic water bottles it'll cost you around $1,500 per year.

Or you could get it from the tap or a public fountain for nothing.

Some folks have wised up. San Francisco has banned disposable plastic water bottles. Closer to home the city of Nanaimo has done the same thing—at least in the city-run recreation centres.

Mind you, in Nanaimo the results have been mixed. The city had hoped the ban would reduce waste, encourage people to bring their own reusable bottles, maybe even promote the use of municipal water. You know, the stuff that gurgles out of taps and water fountains 24 hours a day for free.

Turns out people prefer their plastic-bottled water. "It's kind of ridiculous," says one concession stand owner. "Thirty or forty times per hockey game, I have to explain to people that we're not allowed to sell water."

Well, that's not entirely true. You can buy Perrier water or raspberry-flavoured water but straight H_2O? Not an option.

There are, of course, public drinking fountains in all these facilities but eeew, who wants to drink from *that*?

Besides, it's free, so how good can that be?

Bored, too rich or gullible?

You decide.

We Are Dancing Animals

*H*ere is the opening paragraph of a news story from my morning paper: "Travellers checking into local hotels may be doing so without so much as a 'hello' to a human being next year, according to hoteliers."

The story goes on to explain that hotels are dumping desk clerks and turning that job over to customers' smart phones for check-in, room keys, room service—even to having a room set up exactly the way the customer wants it.

Like, this is a good thing?

Call me a Cro-Magnon but I actually look forward to a smile and a "Can I help you?" from a fellow human when I struggle up to the counter with my reservation in my teeth and my suitcases in tow. I'm in a strange building in a strange town where a strange bed and unfamiliar appurtenances in a strange room await me. I could use some human help.

Plus I don't have a smart phone anyway.

I used to be the second-last person in the world to not own a smart phone. Now I guess I'm last, because Tim Fite finally got one.

"I had resisted for years, but then a friend gave me one," Fite told *New Yorker* magazine. "He told me I was stupid for not having one." Pretty soon Fite was tweeting and texting and playing Angry Birds, just like everyone around him.

Then things got scary. You've heard of phantom limb syndrome, where amputees imagine they feel sensations, even pain, from limbs they no longer have? Tim Fite developed phantom phone syndrome. "I started getting a buzzing in my leg," he said. "It was like the feeling of a call coming in but my phone wasn't even in my pocket . . . Technology wasn't just messing with my time or my productivity. It was messing with my body."

That would never have happened to Kurt Vonnegut, Jr. One day as the author was going out the front door his wife asked him where he was going. Vonnegut said that he was off to buy an envelope. "'Oh,' she says. 'Well, you're not a poor man. Why don't you go and buy 100 envelopes and put them in the closet?'

"And I pretend not to hear her. And go out to get an envelope because I know that I'm going to have a hell of a good time in the process of buying an envelope. I meet a lot of people. And see some great-looking babes. And a fire engine goes by. And I give them the thumbs up. And ask a woman what kind of dog that is. And, and I don't know. The moral of the story is, we're here on Earth to fart around. And of course computers will do us out of that. And what the computer people don't realize, or they don't care, is we're dancing animals. You know, we love to move around."

And Tim Fite? The smart phone addict who suffered from phantom phone syndrome? He's learning to dance again. He's manufactured a rectangular, pocket-friendly, cellphone-like device of fused glass that he sells for $40 a pop. It looks just like a cellphone except it contains no electronics, features no buttons, does not connect to the Internet or do anything else. He calls it the Phoney.

"You can't make a call with the Phoney," explains Fite, "but you can make a point."

Say It Loud!

Whenever I feel my spirits corkscrewing downward from despair over human folly (ISIL, Dick Cheney, Edmonton Oilers) I stop and think of all the wonderful things I never thought I'd live to see.

I never thought I'd see human footprints on the moon.

I never thought I'd see a black man elected to the White House. I never thought I'd hear the CEO of one of the biggest companies in the world stand up and say he was proud to be gay.

That's what Tim Cook did. Specifically, he said, "Let me be clear: I'm proud to be gay, and I consider being gay among the greatest gifts God has given me."

Tim Cook is the Chief Executive Officer of Apple. Can you imagine what a statement like that must mean to a transgendered kid growing up lonely and beleaguered in Wichita or Red Deer—or Toronto, come to that?

We've come a long way, amigos. I grew up in a time when the world was at best frosty toward gays. They weren't even called gay back then. They were homos, queers, fairies and lezzies. The terms weren't used with flat-out hate but there was more than a hint of scorn and derision. Gays were the Other. People who lived in the shadows and spoke a secret language and did God-knows-what with each other.

I spent several years in a Canadian city where the only gay hangout (a cafe on a downtown backstreet) was trashed one Saturday night by a beer-fuelled bunch of Good Old Boys. They swarmed the place with hockey sticks, smashed the windows and threw paint on the walls (it was after hours and no one was there). I don't recall anyone being outraged or marching on city hall. "Oh well," I heard one guy say. "It was just a fag joint."

To go from that era to this in the span of a lifetime—that's pretty amazing. And I haven't even got to talking about K6G.

That's a section of the Los Angeles County Men's Central Jail. The gay section, to be specific. Every inmate in K6G is gay. There is nothing like it in all of America's vast industrial prison complex.

It was created back in 1985 to protect gay prisoners who faced a disproportionate amount of violence from "straight" inmates. What's really amazing is how well it works. There is an overwhelming sense of community among the inmates of the "gay wing." They look after each other. They care. One inmate explained, "For some people, this is their home because a lot of families have disowned them and shunned them, so we're their family."

The irony is that K6G (through the efforts of the inmates, not the staff) does all the things for prisoners that the rest of the prison system so miserably fails to do. It rehabilitates them, gives them a sense of belonging and provides a framework for dealing with the outside world. It is a step forward for civilized behaviour in general.

Too bad people have to go to prison to experience it.

Ah well. Two steps forward, one step back is still a net gain. Meanwhile the CEO of one of the largest companies in the world announces he is proud to be gay and it causes barely a ripple in the notoriously macho stock market.

Onward!

Brace Yourself or I'll Belt You

So Karen at the credit union sees me stroll in, crooks a finger, beckoning me over. (Oh, cripes—did a cheque bounce?)

No. Karen wishes to address my state of dress.

"Suspenders AND a belt, Arthur? That's a sign of a seriously insecure man."

Not guilty. Wearing suspenders and a belt is a sign of a man whose butt has dropped off.

It happens, you know. Cowboys and long-distance truckers have no butts. They hammer them flat with all the bouncing and jouncing their chosen professions entail.

And old guys? We lose our butts too. Collateral damage, along with head hair, high arches and the desire to stay up past 10 p.m.

Calvin Trillin, an old guy who writes for the *New Yorker*, has given a name to the phenomenon. He calls it DST—Disappearing Tush Syndrome. The condition, says Trillin, which "could cause an otherwise respectable senior citizen to walk right out of his pants."

Enter suspenders. An over-the-shoulder weight-bearing device that can hold up a pair of pants regardless of the presence or absence of a fleshy caboose.

The principle of suspenders has been around ever since some saggy-bummed Neanderthal discovered that a shoulder strap knotted to the front and back of his sabre-tooth tiger jockey shorts kept his dangly bits warm and cosy. Suspenders proper didn't show up for another few hundred thousand years—in the mid-nineteenth century, when changes to men's trouser style made belts impractical.

Since then suspenders have had an up and down ride. They became less popular after World War I when men got accustomed to uniform belts. Over the years they swung in and out of fashion, but more out than in. Somewhere along the line they became labelled as underwear, fit only to be seen on lumberjacks, sledge-hammering railroad navvies or tycoons caught with their suit jackets off.

But suspenders fill a need. As all old guys learn when gravity beckons and your butt falls off, belts just won't do the job anymore. Indeed, some health advisors consider reliance on belts to be positively unhealthy. "There are more (bulging) stomachs caused by the wearing of a belt," wrote one Chicago doctor, "than any other one thing that I know of." His advice for achieving that flat-as-a-table abdominal profile? Posture, exercise "and wearing suspenders."

So who took his advice? Well, Annie Hall, in the movie of the same name; Alex, the head hooligan in *A Clockwork Orange*; greed head Gordon Gekko in the movie *Wall Street*; and Larry King, the owl-like celebrity interviewer on television.

And me. But I am not trying to make a fashion statement, break into the movies or host my own TV show. I wear a belt because it gives me a place to hang the pouch of my Swiss Army knife; I wear suspenders to keep my pants up.

My advice to my fellow buttless colleagues: Be not afraid. Hang in there.

And for those who don't like my advice: Belt up.

Part 3

PEOPLE WATCHING

What Money Can't Buy

*L*ate last year Tom Crist, a retired guy in Calgary, got an early Christmas present. It came via a phone call from the folks at Lotto Max; he'd won some money.

No big deal. Tom plays the lotteries regularly and he'd won a few times over the years—10 bucks here, 20 bucks there.

This time was a little different. Tom Crist had won the Lotto Max jackpot—40 million dollars.

Well, we all know how the story unfolds from here. A press conference is called. The winner appears in front of the cameras in a windbreaker and ball cap, smiling shyly next to some Lottery bigwig, both of them standing in front of a cheque blown-up to the size of a highway billboard. The reporters ask the winner what he plans to do with his money. He says he'll maybe paint the garage and pay down the mortgage but he'll keep working his day job down at Acme Screw and Gear.

A few weeks later he's quit his job, bought a whole new wardrobe, a condo in Maui, a champagne-coloured Hummer and a Mazda Miata for the wife.

Except not this time. Tom Crist, it appears, belongs to that rarest of species, the satisfied human.

He's giving the money away. All of it. And not to children,

siblings, cousins, aunts or uncles. He's giving it to charity—cancer research, for starters. "Cancer is a big one," says Tom, "because my wife passed away from cancer two years ago."

But won't he keep a teensy bit—a million or so—just for, you know, mad money? Nope.

"I just retired, so I was fortunate enough to set myself up and my kids anyway, and there was no doubt in my mind where the money was going to go, it was going to charity."

Mr. Crist is not a rich man, you understand. He's just . . . okay. Comfortable. Doesn't need the money.

Is there a word in the English language to describe how refreshing Tom Crist's story is? We live in an age when overfed senators scrabble at the trough to make sure taxpayers are on the hook for their health care and travel claims; where CEOs vie with one another to see how many millions they can personally leverage out of the foundering firms they're supposedly piloting. In my province the BC Ferry Services is awash in a tsunami of red ink; the executives vote themselves huge raises all around. Canada Post regrets that it can no longer afford to provide home delivery for seniors and disabled customers; meanwhile it hobbles along with 22 vice-presidents.

Twenty-two. The entire United States of America, you will recall, makes do with one.

Not that that helps. Thanks to the greed of its own health care providers the richest country in the world cannot deliver even minimal health care coverage for nearly 50 million citizens.

It all comes back to money of course. The stuff that makes the world go round. People say the Bible condemns money as the root of all evil but they're wrong. It's the love of money that causes problems. And as bitch goddesses go it's a mean mother. If you devote yourself to getting rich, you're money hungry. If you're stingy with it, you're a miser. If you splash it around, you're a capitalist pig playboy. If you don't chase it hard enough, you're lazy and unmotivated. If you inherit it, you're a leech and a parasite.

All this for a commodity you can't eat or drink or use to keep off the rain or keep out the cold. Grind up a hundred-dollar bill and smoke it in a hash pipe, you'll only get a headache, not a high.

And yet we all reflexively genuflect before the dollar sign.

Well, most of us do. Not Tom Crist. And among the three of us—Tom, you and me—who do you reckon sleeps best at night?

It's So Gouda to Meet You

*W*hat is the proper response to someone who comes up, extends a hand in greeting and says, "Pleased to meet you. My name is Cheese"?

That is the name nine American couples chose to call their newborns last year, according to a website called BabyCenter.com. And it was by no means the oddest. Other popular names include Hippo, Popeye, Burger, Google and Vanille.

Yes, we are talking about human babies and the names they will have to lug through life.

It's a dangerous gambit, turning to the Internet for assistance in the naming of your child. A couple with the surname McLaughlin asked onliners at namemydaughter.com for a suitable handle to lay on their expected daughter. The front-runner as we go to press is: Cthulhu All-Spark McLaughlin. If it's any consolation Cthulhu (they'll probably just call her Cthul for short) will be coming into a world already well sprinkled with bizarre monikers. David Bowie named his kid Zowie and somewhere in Hollywood there's a woman whose birth certificate reads Moon Unit Zappa. Her father, Frank Zappa, did that to her. One suspects mood-altering substances were involved.

Some countries try to protect the unborn from the loopy

excesses of their parents. In Germany a child's name must by law be not that of "a product, an object, or any other name perceived as absurd or degrading." In Venezuela there is a list of about 100 government-approved names, all of which are gender-specific. Names like Cody, Cory and Dale would be non-starters in Venezuela.

New Zealanders have a law that doesn't allow any names that "may cause offence or lead to bullying" but I don't think the Kiwi name police are all that vigilant. How else to explain the New Zealand man whose name is—deep breath now—Full Metal Havok More Sexy N Intelligent Than Spock And All The Superheroes Combined With Frostnova?

What's more, Mr.—er, Frostnova, is it?—can't even blame his parents. He got saddled as an adult with that name after losing a poker bet. The name change was almost invalidated by another New Zealand statute that forbids names longer than 100 characters.

Luckily, Full Metal Havok More Sexy N Intelligent Than Spock And All The Superheroes Combined With Frostnova comes in at a crisp 99 (including spaces).

Sometimes the naming of children goes badly because of too little imagination rather than too much. That helps to explain why there are a couple of thousand baby girls in New York City alone who answer to the name Fuhmahlee and nearly 4,000 young boys whose first name is Mahlee.

Correction: those are how the names are pronounced. They are spelled "Female" and "Male." Their parents hadn't even bothered to give them a name so the official hospital records used their sex designation as their given name.

Marshall McLuhan once said that naming of a human is a numbing blow from which he or she never recovers.

Marshall McLuhan was a very smart man.

Tinkle, Tinkle Little Star

It's hardly news that every once in awhile substantial segments of the human race go bat poop crazy. That's how we ended up with Great Moments such as the Crusades, the Spanish Inquisition, the Salem witch trials and the German Nazis.

Canadians are not immune. We can surrender to irrational whims and loopy fads with the best of them. That's how we got Trudeaumania, an enduring fan base for the Toronto Maple Leafs and, of course, Ford Nation.

There's a new and viral social craze that's poised to seize our minds and sweep through our ranks, so new it hasn't even been named yet.

May I suggest Whizzteria?

Consider: A young man by the name of Daniel Athens is currently doing a year and a half of hard time in an El Paso jail. His crime: taking a leak against the outside wall of the Alamo. Not only does Mr. Athens get to bed down with murderers, rapists and Aryan Nations goons for the next 18 months, he also has to pay a $4,000 fine. That's the estimated cost to remove evidence of his transgression on the Alamo ramparts. Four thousand dollars??? For peeing outside once? I've been doing that every chance I got my whole life. I must owe somebody a fortune.

Alas, I find increasing evidence that the off-loading of urine and simple common sense no longer live on the same planet. In Portland, Oregon, recently, municipal authorities drained 38 million gallons of water—that's enough to fill 57 Olympic-sized swimming pools—from the city reservoir. Why? Because an 18-year-old kid named Dallas Swonger had been video-taped urinating in it. David Schaff, Oregon's Water Bureau Administrator, harrumphed that, "our customers don't antici-pate drinking water that's been contaminated by some yahoo who decided to pee in a reservoir."

Well, true. But sir? It's not Agent Orange. It's not napalm. It's not radioactive runoff from a Fukushima nuclear reactor.

It's . . . urine. It won't hurt anybody, especially when it's diluted in a ratio of one bladder-full to 38 million gallons of water.

I don't know how to break this to urinophobics like the municipal authorities in Portland or to the El Paso judge, but a substantial number of human beings actually drink the stuff straight. Every day. It's known as urine therapy and adherents claim it's useful for treating everything from gangrene to malaria—also including anemia, hypoglycemia, influenza and the common cold. Some even claim that chugalugging your pee will grow hair on your head and give you a rosy complexion. Most conventional medical practitioners pooh-pooh such claims but they admit drinking your own pee probably won't harm you.

Certainly didn't harm Morarji Desai. The former prime minister of India was a devout believer in urine therapy. He drank an eight-ounce glass of the stuff—straight up, no chaser— every day of his life.

Mind you he did die. Eventually. At the age of 99.

There is one other piece of advice I'd like to pass on for the guardians of that Portland reservoir. You know those geese that swim around in the reservoir? And the ducks and the gulls and the terns? Not to mention the overflying eagles, hawks, sparrows, starlings, herons, chickadees, blackbirds, etc., etc.? Plus of course the otters, raccoons, squirrels, mice and voles that paddle around on the shores of the reservoir?

Ain't a single one of 'em wearing a diaper.

Closest Shave Ever!

*I*n the beginning there was the straight razor. A single blade of finely honed steel that, when folded out of its bone handle and stropped to a keen edge, did a perfectly adequate job of separating a man's whiskers from his jaw.

Unfortunately it had the drawback of being a potentially lethal weapon. For a guy with St. Vitus' dance (or even a hangover) shaving with a straight razor was an enterprise fraught with danger.

So they invented the safety razor—a two-edged blade with a guard plate preventing the user from self-inflicted (well, from *serious* self-inflicted) slashes.

Close shaves with no possibility of slitting one's own jugular: perfect. You'd think Inventor Man would be content to let razor technology rest and move on to finding a formula that turns tar sands into peanut butter. But no, that's not how Inventor Man works.

If guys liked a two-edge razor better than a single-edge blade, it stands to reason they'd go ape bleep for THREE blades, right?

And so in 1998 the technological brainiacs at Gillette came out with the MACH3, which featured not one, not two, but three blades exquisitely cantilevered to nip those budding facial hairs.

The boys in white smocks over at Schick said, "What are we—stropped liver?" and launched the Schick Xtreme3, also a triple blade threat.

This was the hair-removal equivalent of the Russians challenging the Americans to see who could get to the moon first. Razor boffins at both shops pulled out all the stops. Bunsen burners at Gillette labs burned far into the night. Schick spies noted the ominous glow and redoubled their efforts to ensure that Schick, not Gillette, products would reign supreme.

And thus in ensuing years consumers got blitzed with a plethora of products: the Quattro Titanium (Schick) and the Sensor Excel (Gillette), to name only the most prominent.

In 2006 Gillette dropped its hydrogen bomb: the Fusion ProGlide, an instrument that features not just five but SIX blades, baby! The extra is a miniature trailing scythe designed to exfoliate "those tricky spots like sideburns, under the nose and around facial hair."

Six blades to do the job of one. Woody Allen couldn't top that.

Maybe not, but that's not enough to stop the Deep Thinkers over at Gillette. They've just unleashed the all-new ProGlide FlexBall, a razor that features six blades plus an in-handle swivelling ball joint to better follow the contours of the face and to "cut each whisker up to 23 microns shorter."

My question is: Why aren't we giggling? Why aren't the antics of Schick and Gillette technologists fodder for stand-up comedians and the *Rick Mercer Report*?

Simple answer: Because the antics work. Because we're the people gullible enough to pay for bottled water—which comes from the same place that the water in our taps (the free stuff) comes from. We're the people who ooh and aah when Nike announces a new running shoe with a sole so thin "it's like running in your bare feet."

Wow! Just like bare feet. And only a hundred bucks a pair.

I'm going into the razor biz. I plan to market my own model, an all-new, 23-blade, probiotic, gluten-free razor with automatic transmission and power windows. My sales pitch: "Buy Black's Ultimo. Because you'll buy anything."

Our Idiot Quota Overfloweth

*H*ave you heard anything about a national idiot deficiency?

I only ask because a couple of C.I.s (Certified Idiots) have been rapping at Canada's back door asking for a room for the night—or longer.

Glenn Beck, for one. You don't know Glenn Beck? My, you do lead a charmed life. Mr. Beck is an American open mouth radio/TV personality of the knuckle-dragging Neanderthal right persuasion. Each week he broadcasts to his countless drooling fans, bringing fresh reports of socialist hordes massing at the gates eager to destroy the American way of life and probably put lipstick on the Statue of Liberty, too.

An example of Mr. Beck's thought processes can be found in a recent memo he sent out warning that any of his employees caught using an energy-saving light bulb will be fired. "I'm dead serious," he announced. "If anyone does anything in this company because of global warming, they're fired."

Clearly the man is an idiot but that's not what alarms me.

What truly alarms me is that, so fed up is Glenn Beck with the US of A, he's, well, he's . . .

Thinking of moving to Canada.

Please, America, not that. Send us Dick Cheney. Send us

Walter White. Hell, send us what's left of the Soprano mob—you can even return Howie Mandel and Celine Dion, no questions asked. But not Glenn Beck.

And while we've got your attention, America, could you take Ted Cruz off our hands? I realize the Tea Party twit lives in Texas but it seems he was, er, born in Calgary.

I know. We're embarrassed too. If you could see your way clear to slapping Texas plates on his sorry butt, we'd be happy to shred his birth certificate at this end.

Possibly you're worried about what Canada will do for comic relief. Please. Have you met ex-Toronto mayor Rob Ford? Senator Duffy? Stephen Harper in a Stetson at the Calgary Stampede?

We can do our own comic relief, thank you. Speaking of which, a cautionary word about a man who's probably the tallest idiot in your country—Dennis Rodman. Yes, that Dennis Rodman, the ex-basketball dribbler. Dennis isn't hard to spot. He's six foot eight, covered with tattoos, usually has his mouth open and wears green hair plus half a foundry's worth of metal piercings on his otherwise unemployed head. In the last photo I saw of Mr. Rodman he sported two nose rings, at least six lip studs and enough danglies hanging off his ear lobes to qualify as a walking wind chime.

Since his pro basketball career cratered Rodman has appointed himself good-will ambassador to the murderous and medieval North Korean regime of Kim Jong-un. He spends a lot of time in Pyongyang being wined and dined by Killer Kim while ordinary North Koreans perish of starvation outside the palace gates.

So far Rodman hasn't even noticed Canada but I fear he might see a travel brochure that mentions "Kenora, Northern Ontario," misread it as "North Korea" and apply for Canadian citizenship.

That would be even worse than Glenn Beck with a Canadian health care card.

Well, Howdy Stranger

*A*re you feeling blue? Out of sorts? Depressed? Down at the mouth, as it were? Well, here's a thought:

Why don't you get your face paralyzed?

I'm serious. A study conducted by the Georgetown Medical School has found that a significant portion of clinically depressed patients treated with Botox injections showed improved dispositions after the treatment.

The theory (and it is, so far, just a theory) runs something like this: Botox injections in the subjects' foreheads that paralyzed the muscles made it impossible for them to frown. This inability to facially express their depression caused them within a short period of time to "feel" less depressed and eventually improved their spirits.

Sounds woo-woo on the face of it, but it lines up with an evolving school of thought about mental health. The new view suggests that maybe we've got everything backwards. Maybe we don't cry because we're sad; maybe we're sad because we cry. Maybe we don't yell at the kids because we're angry; perhaps we're angry because we yell at the kids. Extending the idea, maybe our brain is subconsciously monitoring our facial expressions and responds by manufacturing the feeling to go with whatever our face is broadcasting to the world.

If that's the case I can save you several hundred bucks not to mention the pain of getting needles in the face. Forget the Botox—just smile.

Really. Right now. Wherever you are, whatever you're doing, just relax and put on a big, face-splitting, earlobe-to-earlobe grin. Hold for 20 seconds.

Now I dare you to try and feel bummed out.

You can't, can you.

If you're feeling really reckless, maintain your smile and say "Hi" to the next stranger you meet.

Not my idea. It belongs to Oprah, who recently launched her Just Say Hello Campaign. "You're telling someone that they exist," she says. "You're telling them that they matter."

Oprah's campaign has been met with a blizzard of scorn and cynicism from several Big City newspaper columnists who like to guard their urban turf from questionable strangers. The ability to be anonymous in a crowd is what makes cities special, they argue. People gravitate to cities to get away from that cloying, small-town, hi-how-are-ya familiarity.

Yeah, well. You say anonymity; I say loneliness.

When I ride the subway and smile at the person across the way I sometimes get a smile back, but more often they look away or even move to another seat—but who's the freak in this situation? I'm just saying "Hi" with my eyes.

Just saying "Hi" is a kind of social magic anyone can master. Sometimes it's all it takes to turn a frown into a smile. Sometimes it's enough to turn somebody's day around.

And it doesn't cost a dime. Try it.

I dare you.

Swastikas? In Ladysmith?

*E*very once in a while I like to escape the gravitational pull of Planet Salt Spring to make a soft landing on what we like to call the Other Island—Vancouver. And one of the places I most especially like to put down is the picturesque town of Ladysmith, population 8,000, give or take. It's a pretty little hamlet that's given itself a facelift, leaving behind its gritty history of coal mining and gussying up to pull in tourists from the Trans-Canada Highway that zips along its doorstep. You find Ladysmith about an hour north of Victoria and 20 minutes south of Nanaimo. The town spreads itself out on a series of geological terraces that descend down to Transfer Beach like giant stair steps. There's a Streets of San Francisco feel to navigating the streets of Ladysmith, followed by a bit of culture shock when you fetch up in front of the Traveller's Hotel, which is one of the many heritage buildings that dot the burg's main street. Look up, way up, past the stone facade of the hotel. See that line of decorated brickwork that wraps around the front of the hotel like a ribbon on a Christmas present? That design in the bricks there . . . isn't that . . . aren't those . . .

Yep. Swastikas. Just like the ones Adolf used to doodle.

You can relax. The Traveller's Hotel in Ladysmith isn't the HQ for Nazis North. The Ladysmith swastikas predate World

War II and so for that matter does the crooked cross itself, by several thousand years, as a matter of fact. The very word derives from ancient Sanskrit: *svastika*, meaning "good" or "auspicious." Swastikas have been found on Neolithic artifacts as well as in India, Asia, the Middle East—even among various First Nations. It's got a fairly rich history here in Canada, too. In the suburbs of Kirkland Lake there's a Swastika United Church; some Canadian postage stamps from the early twentieth century featured swastikas in their borders. Back in the 1920s there was a hockey team in Fernie called the Fernie Swastikas. It's a fine old design the original meaning of which is the polar opposite of everything the Nazis made it stand for. And it's great that the townsfolk of Ladysmith didn't succumb to the misguided chill of political correctness and plaster over the swastikas on their hotel.

Good old Ladysmith. There are lots of good reasons to visit Ladysmith besides the fact that it's Pamela Anderson's hometown.

Check out the funky coffee house, the great bakery, the decidedly eclectic (not to say eccentric) bookstore next to the health food shop. It's all on the main drag, just a loony toss away from the Traveller's Hotel and its garland of swastikas. Be sure to check that out while you're at it. As one Ladysmithian said to me, "Heil Hitler? To hell with Hitler. Ladysmith had the swastikas first."

I Read the News Today, Oh Boy

> *Truth is stranger than fiction because fiction is obliged to stick to possibilities. Truth isn't.*
>
> ANONYMOUS

*A*nd that's the truth. If anyone tried to tell my granddad that, in a couple of generations, folks would be toting a computer, a camera, a calculator, a calendar, a library and a couple of thousand of their favourite tunes all in the same shirt pocket, he'd . . . well, my granddad was never far from his shotgun. You didn't want to startle him with stuff like that.

Just a glance at the front page would give Gramps the vapours. Here's what I found in my newspaper this week:

HAVE WHEELS WILL TRAVEL

Seattle police arrested a man rolling down the street in an office chair last week. Nothing illegal in that, but he was holding a set of drumsticks, had a hubcap strapped to his arm and was wearing motorcycle goggles as well as, according to the police report, "several scarves and purses."

I am not making this up. And speaking of makeup:

BEAUTY TO THE MAX . . . FACTOR

There's a story out of England concerning Charlotte Tilbury, a makeup artist for luminaries including Penelope Cruz, Jennifer

Lopez and Kate Moss. Ms. Tilbury knows her job first hand. She never takes her makeup off. Ever.

Well, okay, maybe when she bathes—but that's the only time and the bathroom door is always locked. She says her husband of six years has never seen her . . . naked, as it were. She gave birth to her son wearing full makeup and she didn't hold her new baby until she had applied her face.

I am still not making this up.

ME, MY ELF AND I

The Supreme Court in Iceland is locked in heady debate over whether a highway project will be allowed to proceed. The problem: the proposed highway threatens to cut through a community and perhaps even destroy a church.

A church for elves.

Icelanders—many of them at any rate—take their elvishness seriously. They call their elves Huldufólk ("hidden folk") and protection of their habitat has affected national planning decisions in the past.

If we could only encourage elves to take up residence in the Northern Gateway pipeline . . .

CEREALLY SURREAL

And from elfies to selfies, meet Mick Hobday, a 33-year-old footloose Brit who's spent the past 10 years (and an estimated $64,000) travelling to 63 countries around the world. Purpose: to take photos of himself eating bowls of cornflakes in exotic settings. Mick reckons he's downed about 4,000 brekkies in this fashion.

Warning: If you get an invitation from Mick to come over and look at his travel slides—don't go.

Wonders of the World

There are more things in heaven and earth, Horatio,
than are dreamt of in your philosophy.

HAMLET

Shakespeare got that right—for Horatio and for the rest of us. Something new and undreamed of dog-paddles into my life virtually every day, whether I'm ready or not. Last week, for instance, I read of a petit contretemps involving an American shopper, a Geneva boutique and a handbag. It seems the American was in the Swiss shop looking around when her eye fell on a particularly fetching purse. "I'd like to see that one, please," she told the clerk.

"No, no, no," the clerk replied briskly. "You don't want to see that one. You want to see this one, because that one will cost too much; you will not be able to afford that."

The American shopper was a black woman. She was also an entrepreneur who earned $77 million last year, according to *Forbes Magazine.*

Perhaps you've heard of her? Oprah Winfrey?

Clearly it was the clerk, not the shopper, who was out of her depth but that's not what amazed me about this story. What stopped me in my tracks was the price tag on the handbag in question.

Thirty-eight thousand dollars.

My mind contracted to a tiny tape loop endlessly repeating *$38,000? You can spend $38,000 for a handbag?*

More things, Horatio . . .

Then I ran across the story of David Rees, who is re-inventing himself as a . . . woodcarver, of sorts. Mr. Rees lives in New York state where he practises—I'm quoting from his website here—"the age-old art of manual pencil sharpening." For a mere $70 Mr. Rees will mail you one professionally sharpened pencil plus a copy of his book, *How to Sharpen Pencils: A Practical & Theoretical Treatise on the Artisanal Craft of Pencil Sharpening for Writers, Artists, Contractors, Flange Turners, Anglesmiths, & Civil Servants.*

Sounds pricey but hey, he throws in a "certificate of sharpening" at no extra charge.

And if that doesn't put lead in your pencil, try this: the Beauty Park Medical Spa in Santa Monica, California, is now offering a procedure called the Male Laser Lift.

We're all familiar with tummy tucks, boob boosts, butt firming and lip enhancement. This is . . . different.

For a mere $575 US, professionals at Beauty Park offer—again, I quote from a website—"a non-surgical male grooming procedure that evens out skin tone, removes discolouration, removes skin tags and provides overall tightening to the external skin."

Down under, if you get my drift.

In the vernacular, the procedure is referred to as "tackle tightening." The actor George Clooney has studied the procedure and he's not impressed—with the procedure or with the way it's described.

Clooney calls it "ball ironing" and he says to hell with it.

I have to line up with Clooney on this one. I'm not opposed to male grooming—if you want to dye your hair, strap yourself into a corset, wear elevator shoes and an aftershave that knocks quail out of the trees at 30 paces, fill your boots, I say.

But steam cleaning the family jewels? Nuts to that.

Goofy for Our Pets

*T*his is an apology to the woman I passed the other morning. I saw the alarm in your eyes, how you clutched your purse and veered around me as if you'd stumbled upon a rabid wolverine.

You'd noticed that while there was nobody with me, I was chatting away. Crooning, actually. Murmuring creepy geezer things like "Aren't you a sweet girl?" and "Oh, what a beauty." I wasn't talking to you, ma'am. I was talking to my dog.

Alarming enough, I suppose. There's no law against addressing Pomeranians, Persians, palominos or parakeets as if they were salient companions capable of a sage and witty retort, but as human behaviour goes it is a touch goofy.

Guilty as charged. My old girl is thirteen and a half, cloudy of eye and stiff of gait but her tail still wags when she sees me and that is reward enough to risk looking ridiculous.

All pet owners carry the ridiculous gene, some more openly than others. We give our pets silly names and brag about their "human" qualities.

Often the gene doesn't really kick in until our pet kicks off. Disposing of a pet's remains can trigger some truly bizarre behaviour. A lucky few get to repose in a shady spot under the backyard apple tree; others occupy an urn on the mantle.

Or there's the Celestis option. Celestis is a Houston enterprise specializing in flights into space. For a mere $995 US Celestis will load your pet's ashes into a rocket and fire them into eternal orbit around the earth.

Too remote for you? Then consider engaging the services of Dutch artist Bart Jansen and inventor Arjen Beltman. They can transform your taxidermied pet into a radio-controlled drone.

Don't laugh. When Jansen's pet cat Orville expired in 2012 he had him stuffed and fitted with wings and a motor. As I write, the Orvillecopter is hovering somewhere over Amsterdam.

That's creepy, even by delusional pet owners' standards. Much better to spoil your pet when he, she or it is alive.

Which must be how the Halvorsen family of Lillestrom, Norway, felt when they decided to take an extended vacation in Thailand. They couldn't take their bulldog, Igor, but they fretted that he would feel abandoned, even traumatized. So they hired a carpenter to construct a replica of the family living room and install it at a commercial kennel. The walls of the fake room were painted the same shade of grey. They found a matching coffee table, even installed the family chesterfield, plus of course Igor's favourite bed, pillow, blanket and toys.

Was Igor fooled? Hard to say. He spent most of his time at the boarding kennel goofing around outside with his new BFF—a Saint Bernard named Helga.

The pet/owner dynamic is a puzzling one. Sometimes it's hard to figure out which party got the brains.

Justice Blind? Nearsighted For Sure

*T*rivia question: What do you call that bowl thingy full of holes that lives in the kitchen cupboard, the one that looks like a basin that's been peppered with shotgun pellets?

Time's up. It's a colander—a sieve, basically. It's used for draining water off pasta and rice and such.

Or you can be like Obi Canuel and wear it on your head.

Obi Canuel (real name) of Vancouver wears a colander and he's vexed that the Insurance Corporation of British Columbia won't let him pose for his driver's licence photograph while so adorned.

It's a religious thing for Obi. He's a practising Pastafarian, you see. He belongs to the First Church of the Flying Spaghetti Monster and I swear I am not making any of this up.

He feels that his rights under the Canadian Charter of Rights and Freedoms are being violated by ICBC's ruling and he may have a case. ICBC policy guarantees that no one will be asked to remove headgear that doesn't interfere with facial recognition technology "as long as it is worn in conjunction with religious practice."

I've seen a photograph of Obi in costume. He looks reasonably normal. Aside from that colander on his head.

Naturally he's planning to sue.

Good luck with that, Obi. The Canadian system of justice is weird and capricious, and not just when it comes to religious headgear.

You can go to jail for an overdue library book or you can be like Ian Thow, a BC con artist who stole millions by bilking hundreds of old-age pensioners out of their life savings. For his sins Thow went ever-so-briefly to jail in 2010 but in less than two years he was out and at last report soaking up sunshine in Mexico.

That's how our justice system rolls, baby. A single roach in your car ashtray can earn you a lifetime criminal record, or you could be like Michael Simoneau-Meunier, a two-bit thug doing time in Quebec's Bordeaux Prison for various violent acts including permanently disabling an innocent bystander with a baseball bat. M. Simoneau-Meunier recently posted a selfie on Facebook with a bottle of cognac in one hand and a giant spliff in the other. "Livin' da jail life," it was entitled, and yes, he was in jail when the photo was taken.

Ah well, the law isn't always an ass. At least that pusher in Lethbridge who was dealing coke out of his school locker finally got nailed.

Actually, he wasn't a drug dealer. He was Keenan Shaw, a Grade 12 student. And the coke he was dealing wasn't even Coke. It was . . . Pepsi. As in Pepsi-Cola. Keenan (an aspiring capitalist if every there was) was selling pop to fellow students who were too lazy or impatient to wait until they were off school grounds to buy it. Officials at Winston Churchill High School slammed Keenan with a two-day suspension. "We can't have just anyone coming into the school and selling anything they want," explained a school superintendent.

Bang on. Now, free marketeering while in prison, that's a different story.

Pepsi-Cola in high school; Rémy Martin cognac in jail. Who said Justice was blind?

And what's it cost to become a Pastafarian?

Embear-assing Behaviour

I consider Winnie the Pooh to be one of the noblest gifts Canada ever bestowed on the rest of the world. And make no mistake: Winnie is Canadian. As Canadian as moose antlers, Murray McLaughlin and Margaret Atwood all wrapped up in a Don Cherry sports jacket.

Yes, I know that Winnie the Pooh is an imaginary creature, "a fictional anthropomorphic teddy bear," as my dictionary so disdainfully sniffs. But Winnie was a real fur-and-blood Canadian bear. He was born in the backwoods of Northwestern Ontario in the early part of the last century and sold as a cub on the White River train platform to a Canadian soldier who was bound for Europe to fight in World War I. The soldier, Lieutenant Harry Colbourn of Winnipeg, was deployed along with his furry mascot to England.

When it came time for Lieutenant Colbourn to go to the front, "Winnie" (so named after the lieutenant's hometown) was donated to the London Zoo where he lived out his life, but not before captivating a little boy's imagination—and more importantly, that of the little boy's father, the writer A.A. Milne.

In a way, Winnie the Pooh personified the Canadian

stereotype. He was friendly, helpful, steadfast, powerful but pacific and perhaps a touch *provincial* for the world stage.

Okay, Winnie was gullible and naive. "A bear of little brain," as his creator would write. Think Bob and Doug McKenzie with fur.

What Winnie the Pooh never was is X-rated—but try to tell that to Poland. A statue of Winnie the Pooh has been banned from a playground in the Polish town of Tuszyn.

Why? Because he doesn't wear underpants, that's why. Winnie is bear-assed, if you will.

"The problem with that bear is it doesn't have a complete wardrobe," explained one town councillor. "It is half-naked, which is totally inappropriate for children."

You know, I never thought of it before but the councillor is right. I've never seen Winnie wearing anything more than a red T-shirt and sometimes a little toque on his head. Shows what a gullible and naive Canuck I am, I guess.

The Polish guardians of public sanctity may have started an international shaming storm for fantasy bears. Already the British Board of Film Classification has been moved to slap a WARNING tag on *Paddington* (a movie about another half-dressed bear). The board says the film contains "dangerous behaviour, mild threats, mild sex references and mild bad language," rendering it "unsuitable for children under eight."

Paddington Bear? Really????

I don't want to panic the good citizens of Poland or Britain but have they noticed the nether quarters of Donald, Daisy and Daffy Duck? Mickey and Minnie? Frosty the Snowman?

If they can't handle cartoon semi-nudity they definitely should stay out of the Canadian backwoods.

Our bears don't even wear T-shirts.

Part 4

THAT'S DR. BLACK, IF YOU DON'T MIND

How a Can-do Fella Gets Things Done

*A*s a mostly retired guy I get to spend a lot of time on chores and projects I never seemed to get around to when I was nine-to-fiving it. Naturally I try to bring the same level of professional efficiency to these non-paying pastimes as I did to my job. We're not splitting the atom here, or solving the Middle East conflict. The key is simple, no-nonsense, day-to-day organization. That's why each night before I turn in I sit down and make out a To-Do list. Here, for instance, is my To-Do list for today:

1. Do stretching exercises
2. Paint garden gate
3. Groom dog
4. Change oil in car
5. Weed flowerbed
6. Pay bills

Now, I wasn't born yesterday. I know that life is unpredictable and circumstances change. A guy needs to be flexible and creative if a guy expects to get anything accomplished. A guy can't just blindly charge down the field if somebody moved the goalposts overnight. This morning, for instance, turns out to be grey and overcast. You can practically smell rain in the air. That means I can kiss goodbye my plans for flowerbed weeding and garden gate repairing. Fortunately (here comes that flexible, adaptive quality I mentioned) I have backup: an emergency list of To-Do chores to fill such gaps, which I can smoothly incorporate into the daily flow. So we have a rain delay? What a magnificent opportunity to take care of a chore from my reserve list, like . . . sure! The weekend crossword puzzle! That's been preying on my mind since Saturday. What's a five-letter word for HIJKLMNO?

1. Finish crossword puzzle

Well, that took a little longer than I expected. The answer is "water"—H to (2) O—get it? Neither did I. I had to Google it. And since I was already at the keyboard I decided to

2. Check email

Which also took longer than expected. (Have you seen that video where the basking shark comes up right under the tour guide's kayak? Never get tired of watching that.)

Anyway, no point getting up to my elbows in used engine oil right before lunchtime, so scratch the oil change. And I'd be way too uncomfortable doing stretching exercises on a full belly, so skip that too. On to Alternative Chore number three:

3. Check email

Oh. Already did that. Well, no harm in seeing if anything new came in . . .

Cripes, where does the time go? It didn't rain after all. In fact it's full sun in the garden now. Baaaad time to paint the gate. Pretty sure I read that paint won't set properly if it's too hot. That leaves: groom dog.

You've heard the saying "let sleeping dogs lie," right? Lot of wisdom in those old adages. I had the brush and the comb and the clippers all ready to go when I spied my dog flaked out and snoring under the hammock. Under the—unoccupied—hammock.

4. Road test outdoor sleeping facility

I'm not going to lie to you. I took a little break there. Oh, I could have taken care of the bill-paying chore, but come on—in weather like this? You can't lie in a hammock in January, you know. Best to make hay while the sun shines, as they say. Or in this case, saw logs. Just a quick 40 winks listening to the birds and the drone of a faraway lawn mower (not mine).

Actually, a little more than 40 winks I guess. As a matter of fact, the sun's going down and it's getting cool. I could probably get those bills paid after supper, except the Monty Python reunion special is on cable tonight. According to the *TV Guide* it's three hours long.

That'll leave me just enough time to make out my To-Do list for tomorrow.

Need a Password? Take Mine

*D*ear Cyberthieves Out There:

The first thing I want you to know is that you don't scare me.

Your latest scam—this Heartbleed computer bug that's got security experts going cyber-squirrelly? Advising us to "change all your passwords for everything," as one nervous nerd advised?

Forget it. I'm not doing that. Not because I'm computer savvy (hah!) or feeling devilishly defiant. The fact is, I've already used all the passwords I can handle. My mental password floppy disc is full. I've used my mother's maiden name, my father's middle name, my high school nickname, the name of my first dog, last cat and only parrot. I've combined them with my birthdate, my wedding anniversary, the square root of my childhood street address, my telephone number (backwards) plus a series of capital letters, not to mention #, $, @, %, & and * inserted randomly, followed by the married name of the third male cousin on my wife's side. Want to hear my last password? BowSer52!!Minnie5805//(yrpla-ceormine)198FOUR. Take it. Run with it. Fill your cyberboots.

That's just my latest password, you understand. Obedient little cybersucker that I am, I've been changing them every six months. When that became too mentally challenging I started rotating them regularly so that last month's Facebook password became this month's Linkedin password, which would be relegated to next month's Gmail account and . . .

Yeah, well. That, too, became cumbersome, so I invented this new system where I wrote out all my passwords in ballpoint and Scotch taped the list to the wall beside my computer. Perfect! I had them all in one place where I could find them when I needed them. I showed off my new system to the Resident Critic. "How's that for handy and innovative?" I crowed. She rolled her eyes and remarked, "So now anyone who wants your passwords just has to walk into your office and steal this list?"

After pointing out to Resident Critic that sarcasm is not an attractive character attribute, I fell to musing about her observation.

And that's when the scales fell from my eyes.

Why, I asked myself, do I have all these stupid passwords? Why do I have any passwords at all? I'm not a CSIS agent or a dope dealer. I'm not a secret porn troller or a pedophile.

Online banking? I don't indulge. I subscribe to this antediluvian habit of actually going to my bank and interacting with a human (we used to call them "tellers"). We banter, I get a free smile—sometimes two—and she has to do the math.

It's a great system, and I don't have to remember an eight-digit, purposely randomized cryptic and confusing Open Sesame code. I just have to remember what street the bank is on.

So I guess this column is an open letter to everyone in cyberspace. Please don't send me anything if it requires a password. I'm not playing that game anymore. The only password I'm retaining is my email handle and that's easy: rufus@saltspring.com.

Feel free to use that, copy it or sell it to that guy in Nigeria who's keen to send me $36 million.

You'd rather do face-to-face? That's easy too.

You can find me in the bank lineup most Monday mornings.

Say It Loud, Say It Proud: I'm Shy

They've just found a gene for shyness. They would have found it earlier but it was hiding behind a couple of other genes.

JONATHAN KATZ

Ah yes, shyness. It would be hilarious if it wasn't so . . . excruciating. I speak as a certified Shy Guy. Sure, I'm the clown who talks too loud, warbles off-key and has been known to wear a lampshade for a fedora. It's all just an act to cover up my basic shyness. Shy people are not welcome in our society. Well-meaning friends devise plots to "bring us out of our shells" and get us to "assert ourselves." Type A personalities call us wusses, chicken bleeps, even cowards.

T'ain't true, but we're too shy to correct our detractors.

In China shyness is seen as a welcome and respected character trait. There it bespeaks a person who thinks before he/she acts, someone who has control of their impulses and behaves rationally rather than emotionally.

Different story on this continent where we don't place much value on introspection. Gasbags like Don Cherry get celebrity status; thinkers like Michael Ignatieff get the boot. The Bible claims the meek are blessed. Try to prove it at a hockey game or on the floor of the Toronto Stock Exchange.

The worst thing about shyness? Opportunities missed. Shy people don't go for the brass ring. And that's a shame—especially when the brass ring isn't so far out of reach. James Matthew Barrie, the man who gave us Peter Pan, was pathologically shy. Invited to a dinner with A.E. Housman he sat mute beside him—even though he'd longed to meet the famous poet for a long time. Afterwards Barrie wrote this letter:

> Dear Professor Houseman, I am sorry about last night, when I sat next to you and did not say a word. You must have thought I was a very rude man: I am really a very shy man. Sincerely yours, J.M. Barrie.

Housman wrote back:

> Dear Sir, I am sorry about last night, when I sat next to you and did not say a word. You must have thought I was a very rude man: I am really a very shy man. Sincerely yours, A.E. Housman.
>
> P.S. And now you've made it worse for you've spelled my name wrong.

I'll leave the last word to another man of letters, Garrison Keillor, who had to overcome painful shyness to become the bestselling author and storytelling genius that he is. But he never forgot (or vanquished) his shyness. In the end he decided he doesn't want to. Keillor wrote: "Shyness is not a disability or a disease to be overcome. It is simply the way we are. And in our own quiet way we are secretly proud of it."

Amen to that. I'm shy—wanna make something of it?

Let Me Sign That For You

I've never built a chicken coop. My vegetable garden is a panoramic showroom of weeds, exotic and mundane. I am congenitally unable to sing a cappella, dance the fandango, play the viola or drive a golf ball. I can't remember whether the red or the black booster cable goes on the positive or the negative battery thingy. I have to ask small children on the street to stop the beeping of my wristwatch. I can't, in short, actually do anything.

Except write.

Books, mostly. Eighteen of them, I think (I can't count either). But write books I do, and certain aspects of the experience remain just as opaque as the workings of my TV remote or the female mind.

Such as signing the title page. Why do some people want me to sign copies of my book? I went across the country (to Halifax, in fact) last year to sit in a bookstore window and chat with book buyers while I signed their copies of my latest book. (*Fifty Shades of Black*, Douglas & McIntyre. Better bookstores everywhere.)

Why? My name is already on the cover of the book and you can actually read it, unlike my turkey-scratch signature. What possible value does my doodle, scrawled in ballpoint, add to the item in question?

It wasn't always so. Before the twentieth century no one expected an author to actually write his signature on a copy of his book. Books then were simply inscribed "from the author." But I suppose someone realized that any bookstore clerk could write that phrase on an inside page and no one would be the wiser, so a bona fide author's signature became de rigueur.

Which led to a whole literary sub-industry, not to mention some nifty book-signing stories. Back in the 1970s Richard Nixon (remember him?) wrote an autobiography called *Six Crises*. Doing the obligatory book signing in a Washington bookstore, Nixon asked a purchaser to whom he should address the inscription. The book buyer replied, "You've just met your seventh crisis. My name is Stanislaus Wojechzleschki."

About the same time one of the great literary feuds in American history was playing out. Staunch right-winger William F. Buckley and blazing liberal Norman Mailer professed to hate one another's guts, but one suspects there was sneaking admiration on at least one side of the firefight. Buckley certainly thought so. He sent a copy of his autobiography to Norman Mailer but puckishly declined to sign it. Flummoxed, the notoriously egotistical Mailer thumbed through the index at the back of the book to see if he'd been mentioned in the text. Right beside "MAILER, Norman" he found a note in Buckley's handwriting. It read, "Hi, Norman."

Signing one's books can be an exercise in ego deflation. The composer Aaron Copland was at the checkout counter in a bookstore one day when he noticed a woman buying a copy of his book, *What to Listen for in Music*, along with a paperback edition of Shakespeare's *A Midsummer Night's Dream*. He sidled up to the woman and asked, "Would you like me to autograph your book?"

"That would be lovely," the woman beamed. "Which one?"

I Ran with the Bulls—No Bull

You don't hear much about Saint Fermin—unless you live in Pamplona, that is. The man who would become Saint Fermin was born in that Spanish city about 17 centuries ago. He became bishop of his hometown and embarked on a cross-border tour to spread the gospel to the heathen French. Who beheaded him for his trouble.

Gone, but not completely forgotten—especially in Pamplona in July when celebrants from around the world take part in the Fiesta de Sanfermines, a two-week bacchanalia during which participants sing, dance, get drunk . . .

And then run with the bulls.

Six Iberian fighting bulls and every one of them a mean mother. To compare the Spanish fighting bull to the dozy, cud-chewing Holstein or Hereford variety is like comparing a Porsche Spyder to a cross-town bus. The Iberian bull is One Huge Muscle. It can outrun a horse in 100 metres, turn on a five-peseta piece and fears nothing on this earth including locomotives, horses and us bipeds.

It goes without saying that only an idiot would be stupid enough to get out in front of such critters and try to outrun them, right?

Hello, my name is Idiot. I ran with the bulls. Twice.

This, of course, was back when I was young, fit and even stupider than I am today. So stupid that I didn't realize that the dice are actually loaded in favour of the bulls. It works like this: Each morning of the fiesta six new bulls are corralled in front of Pamplona's city hall. The dopes who have elected to "run with the bulls" are similarly corralled 400 metres down a narrow, snake-like street. A cannon fires and the bulls are released at the same time as the barrier comes down for the runners. Everybody—bulls and runners—now takes off for the bullring, which is another 400 metres down the aforementioned twisty road. Oh, and all side streets are blocked off. If you run with the bulls, you've got to go the distance.

Well, big deal. Who can't run 400 metres? Have I mentioned how fast the Iberian bulls are? I hadn't even covered half the distance when I heard the unmistakable staccato beat of hoofs coming fast. I looked back and saw a wall of wicked-looking horns coming my way.

What did I do? I made an immediate right turn and slammed myself into a stone wall, which I hugged closer than a sailor with a five-dollar taxi dancer. The wall was whitewashed; so was my complexion. The bulls ignored me. I think protective colouration saved my life.

The next year I was a little wiser (though still dumb enough to do it again). I trained by doing wind sprints. I sharpened my elbows Gordie Howe style to help me hack my way through slower runners. When the cannon went off I ran like a cheetah on meth.

I got to the bullring long before any other runner—so quickly in fact that the crowd in the stands whistled a personal greeting to me.

While I was taking bows an American came up and whispered that actually whistling is the Spanish form of the baseball raspberry. They weren't cheering my entrance; they were booing my cowardice.

Still . . . in the past 90 years fifteen runners have been gored to death at the fiesta. Dozens are injured every year. As a matter of fact, Bill Hillman took a horn through the thigh last year. He's the author of a book called *Fiesta: How to Survive the Bulls of Pamplona.*

I imagine he spent his recuperation working on a sequel.

Have Train Ticket, Will Travel

I am the Joe Btfsplk of travel. You know Joe B.? A cartoon character in the L'il Abner comic strip. Joe was a jinx. He carried around his personal black cloud of bad luck, which you could be infected by if you stood too close to Joe.

Ditto for me when it comes to tourism. If you see me coming toward you in Tilley shorts and sunglasses, lugging a backpack and a boarding pass, drop your bags and run far away. If we travel together you will suffer from altitude sickness, mislaid passports, drunken taxi drivers, phantom hotel reservations and your luggage will likely end up in a Somali war zone.

Consider: I went to Hawaii; it snowed. I went to the sunny, arid Canary Islands; it rained for 11 days straight. I've been hustled in Havana, bamboozled in Bangkok, marooned in Morocco and pickpocketed in Panama.

But I'd never ridden VIA Rail's *Canadian* from Vancouver to Toronto. What could go wrong—they're professionals, right? VIA trains have been criss-crossing the country in gleaming, purring, clickety-clacking stainless steel convoys since forever. Everyone knows about the impeccable service, the spotless linen, the sparkling, actual silverware (not the crappy plastic Barbie spoons you get on airplanes).

And there's the scenery. My train started in Vancouver, meandered leisurely through the saw-toothed Rockies, glided smoothly across the Big Sky Prairies, which yielded to the rock-trees-lake-rock-trees motif of northern Ontario, which gradually morphed and melded into gorgeous Group of Seven landscapes of Muskoka cottage country and finally, Toronto.

Eventually. But this time Joe Btfsplk was on board. We made it to Edmonton before the infamous Btfsplk mojo began to assert itself. By Wainwright we were running two hours late. Mechanical problems. We lost more time between Watrous and Melville, Saskatchewan, after a passenger hit her head on a footrest, sustaining, the conductor assured me, a clip on the forehead that "looked like a horse kicked her." The next passenger to fall didn't suffer his (mild) heart attack until we'd left Gogama, Ontario, but it took some adroit cellphone manoeuvring to find a meeting point so an ambulance could pick him up and take him to a hospital. Not that we were in a hurry. One of the train's engines had gone to locomotive heaven by that time and the remaining engine, overheating with the strain of lugging that corpse plus the other 10 cars, meant we had to stop every 80 kilometres to check for overheating bearings.

And eventually we had to unhitch and ditch the dead engine. That ate up another hour.

And then there's the little secret the brochures don't mention. VIA rents the track from CN Rail. CN is in the freight business. That means boxcars first, passengers last. On Day Three we stopped 13 times to cede freight trains the right of way. It eats up a lot of minutes, slowing a big train to a stop, coasting into a lay-by while a freight train passes, then getting up to speed again. Soon we were running seven hours late.

But kudos to VIA Rail personnel. They are consummate pros in the hospitality biz. With loving kindness they transformed a simmering miasma of passenger anger to a near-ethereal plane of philosophical What's the Rush. They treated us like family. Like a family of rajahs. They cajoled, they commiserated, they all but stroked our brows with Evian-dampened VIA serviettes.

The free champagne they kept doling out didn't hurt either.

Our train limped into Toronto's Union Station 12 hours and 20 minutes late. We should have been a cauldron of red-faced, cursing, pissed-off customers. I didn't hear or see a single one. It was an "adventure." An "experience." A "lot of fun." There were smiles and hugs all around.

Plus every passenger received a 100 percent discount on the economy fare of their next VIA Rail trip.

Even Joe Btfsplk.

Thanks, VIA Rail—but letting Joe on your train again? You're playing with fire.

Having the Write Stuff

*P*leased to meetcha. What do you do?

Well, I'm a writer.

No, I mean what do you do for a living?

I can't count the number of times I've endured variations of that conversation. Even my mammy thought scribbling for a living was an insane way to try to pay the rent. I never signed up to be a writer but writing is about all I've done by way of work for the past 40 years, so I guess a writer is what I am.

There are more lucrative ways to bring home the back bacon. Writers don't get paid like corporate lawyers or investment counsellors—or like third-line defencemen for the Anaheim Ducks, come to that.

On the other hand, there are perks. No dress code to fret about. Your morning commute only runs from the coffee pot to your computer. You set your own hours—no boss looking up with a glare as you fling yourself at your desk fifteen minutes after nine.

It's a pretty decent gig, writing is, but I'll tell you what it isn't.

Glamorous. Writing is definitely lax in the glamour category.

It's one of life's dirty little tricks: To be a writer you have to be open and sensitive to the world around you but to sell your writing you have to be about as sensitive as Rob Ford on a bender.

Otherwise the experience will crush you like a fruit fly.

Consider: last year I flew from Victoria to Halifax to do a reading at the opening of a new city library. Coast to coast. That's getting on for 5,000 kilometres. Double that since I had to turn around and fly back the next day. Still, it's good publicity for my book and the Halifax Library patrons have a good rep for buying books at readings. And sure enough it's a full house when I show up—at least 200 people! They're cheerful, enthusiastic. I can just tell they're going to buy wagonloads of my books . . .

As they might have, had any of my books shown up for sale.

They didn't. Bookseller screw-up? Publisher snafu? Canada Post black hole? Dunno. Nobody ever got back to me.

Did I blow a gasket? Nah. Spiral into despair? Pah. I'm used to it. To flog books in Canada is to subject yourself to a Turkish steam bath of humiliation. I have faced an audience of three at a bookstore in Edmonton. I have resisted the urge to strangle a TV host who opened with, "This new book of yours . . . what's it about?"

I have sat cheek by jowl with Robert Bateman, the famous artist, as we signed copies of our new books at adjoining tables.

Well, correction. Bateman signed copies of his new book— great teetering stacks of them as fans lined up out the door and down the street for the chance to give him their money. I watched Bateman as the ink in my virgin ballpoint dried up and turned to blue crust.

Then there was the time I read to a service club in Vancouver. Most of the audience was enthusiastic save for a gent in a three-piece suit. He never cracked a smile; kept looking at his watch. He looked like he desperately wanted to be someplace else.

As he was leaving I asked if I'd offended him. He said no, but he'd thought the evening's speaker was Conrad Black.

Sorry, pal. As a writer I've dangled gerunds, mangled metaphors, even butchered an allusion or two, but my record's clean. No priors here.

Just Put Your Lips Together

"You know how to whistle, don't you? You just put your lips together and blow."

That's Lauren Bacall in *To Have and Have Not* murmuring perhaps the sexiest two sentences in the history of Hollywood cinema. As a hormone-besotted teenager I was paralyzed when I watched that scene unfold on the big screen.

And I wasn't even sure what she was talking about.

Oh, I knew about whistling—a simple act (just put your lips together and blow, stupid) but with unknowable consequences. There was that time, for instance, that whistling almost got me killed.

I was 16 years old, working as a deckhand aboard the S.S. *Federal Monarch*, an oil tanker bound from Dartmouth, Nova Scotia, to Venezuela. I was hustling along the deck, off to daub some paint on a lifeboat, whistling, if memory serves, "Oh Susanna," when a hand attached to a muscular brown arm came out of nowhere and grabbed me by the jaw.

"What you doin' mon?" asked the voice behind the arm. It belonged to the ship's bo's'n, a burly Jamaican named Archie. My mouth was too scrunched up in his hand to do anything more than mumble.

"You whistle on dis ship again, I slit you t'roat."

He was smiling when he said it but he sported a wicked-looking hooked knife on his belt and if it was a bluff, I wasn't about to call it. Nor would I whistle on that ship, or any ship, ever again. Turns out that sailors are a deeply superstitious lot, and whistling is considered to be an invitation to the gods to sink your vessel.

Just put your lips together and blow. That's all Bing Crosby did in his recording of "White Christmas," but the man played his lips like Louis Armstrong blew trumpet. He whistled a solo that's engraved on the memories of millions. Just by putting his lips together.

Back in the 1960s I met a couple of Canucks who had spent a month on La Gomera, one of the Canary Islands off the coast of Africa. They'd hiked to the top of an island mountain and were baffled because the people they met along the way always seemed to be expecting them.

When they reached the top of the mountain, villagers were gathered around an open fire where a goat had been killed and roasted for them. A feast had been prepared. Understand that this was long before cellphones and Wi-Fi. La Gomera was an exceedingly rural island. Most of the inhabitants had no electricity or telephones.

What they shared instead was a phenomenon called Silbo Gomero. It's a language consisting of two vowels and four consonants that could be combined to make some 4,000 "words"—all of them whistled.

News of the *extranjeros* had been passed along ahead of them by whistle telegraph, islanders just putting their lips together and blowing.

There's a teenager named Walker Harnden down in North Carolina who's only 19 years old but he's already in the *Guinness Book of Records*. He got there by putting his lips together and blowing the highest note ever recorded (B7 in case you want to give it a shot).

Harnden admits that he "whistles all the time"—up to four or five hours a day.

A lucky thing for the kid that he never went to sea.

The Woodchopper's Bawl

I come to sing the praises of a simple, even brutish, habit of mine. As a pastime it is physically exhausting, mind-numbingly repetitive, potentially limb threatening, and eco-ethically tainted if not downright impure.

It is chopping wood.

There is an ancient Chinese proverb that says: chop your own wood and it will warm you twice. I once repeated that to an old Finlander I knew in Thunder Bay. He smiled and shook his head. "Seven times," he said. "It heats you seven times."

Once, he said, when you trekked out into the bush to find a likely tree. Twice when you chopped it down. Three times when you trimmed the branches and bucked it up into rounds. Four times when you hauled it back to the house. Five times when you unloaded it in your yard. Six times when you split and stacked it. Seven times when you lugged an armful into the house, put it in the stove and lit the fire.

"Seven times," old Charlie Pelto nodded and winked at me. "Good deal."

There are some simple truths you learn while chopping wood. Soft wood splits less cleanly than hard. Dull axes are dangerous.

Don't try to chop through a knot. Wear eye protection. Dry wood splits better than green.

Except . . .

Where I live there is a beautiful deciduous tree called the arbutus (madrona to Yanks). When it's dry it burns like a dream— hot and bright, with almost no ash residue. You don't want to try and burn it when it's green but that's when you want to split it. Green arbutus is a woodchopper's wet dream. It flies apart at the bite of an axe. Swinging your axe at a piece of arbutus that's dried out is like trying to chop a cement block crossed with a rubber traffic pylon.

Eco-purists look askance at the practice of burning wood for warmth and, by extension, at the act of chopping wood to do it. They have a point. Woodsmoke undeniably pollutes the air and falling ash besmirches the landscape.

So sue me. I am in love with the smell of woodsmoke and I can think of few more cheery, life-affirming sights than a curlicue of grey smoke undulating up from a house chimney against a backdrop of Canadian winter sky.

I haven't even mentioned that ultimate woodchopper's payoff—the rosy, drowsy-making glow of a roaring, well-laid fire. That's a pleasure you'll have difficulty extracting from your electric baseboard heater—or your solar panel, come to that. A good fire is close to good sex. A fellow by the name of Charles Dudley Warner once said, "To poke a wood fire is more solid enjoyment than almost anything in the world."

Mr. Warner was right, but first you have to get the wood into the fireplace. Now if you'll excuse me, I've got a cord of green arbutus in my front yard that's crying for attention. As the Inuit say, "Yesterday is ashes, tomorrow is wood. Only today does the fire burn brightly."

But only after you chop the wood.

The Doctor Is a Fake

*O*nce in a while—about every six months or so—a letter drops through my mail slot addressed to "Dr. Arthur Black."

It's true. I am a doctor. Have been for about the past 20 years. And it embarrasses the hell out of me.

I don't deserve the title of doctor. I couldn't stitch somebody's leg up or diagnose a sprain or decode an X-ray chart. Cripes, it's all I can do to prise the lid off an aspirin bottle.

But that's not the kind of doctor I am. My field of expertise is much more useless than that. I am a Doctor of Letters.

Whatever that means.

In my case it means that sometime toward the end of the last century a university I never attended decided to confer an honorary degree on me. All I had to do was show up on Convocation Day dressed like a transvestite with a black pizza box balanced on my head and give a speech.

Hey, presto! A doctor was born.

I gave a pretty good speech if I do say so but it was hardly the equivalent of eight years of study and practice that most doctors put in before they get their diploma. And yet, if I cared to, I could have cards printed up with "Doctor" in front of my name. I could perhaps enhance my chances with reservations clerks by letting it be known that they were dealing with Dr. Black, not some doofus who usually wears a ball cap and running shoes.

I don't. With my luck I'd just be checking in to a hotel as Dr. Black when the guy in line behind me would turn purple, swoon and do a face plant. Someone would sing out, "IS THERE A DOCTOR IN THE HOUSE?" and the check-in clerk would point at me.

"Yes, well, not really. That is, I AM a doctor but . . ."

Mind you there are a lot of fake doctors out there who really do ride their trophy credentials in the hope of gaining some kind of social prestige. In my experience the more a person talks about being a doctor, the less chance he or she is a doctor of anything useful.

And even at that, being a doctor doesn't automatically confer respect. I know a heart surgeon who went to pick up his motor-cycle from a garage he'd taken it to for a tune-up. The mechanic who worked on his bike smirked as he wiped his hands with a cloth. "You know, doc, we're pretty much in the same line of work. I took the cylinder head off your bike this afternoon. That's like a heart. I open it up, take the valves out, fix 'em, put 'em back in and it purrs like a kitten. So how come you get the big bucks and I get chicken feed when we do the same work?"

The surgeon smiled and said, "Try doing it while the engine is running."

Part 5

THE DAZE OF OUR LIVES

Everything Old is New Again

I'm walking through a shopping mall with my son when we encounter a guy who looks like he's on his way to an early Halloween party. He's wearing goggles and a World War I leather flying helmet. Also purple suspenders over a banker's vest. Below that he's sporting vintage Mountie trousers that end at his knees with laces. He has high leather boots on his feet to complete the costume.

I try not to stare. "What the hell was THAT?" I mutter to my son after the vision has passed. My son does that eye-roll thing that young people do when old farts say something stupid and out of it.

"Steampunk," he explains. *Steampunk? What the hell is THAT?*

Steampunk turns out to be yet another fashion sub-genre that somehow managed to appear and thrive without my ever being aware of it. It has its origins in science fiction circa the early 1900s—H.G. Wells' *Time Machine* kind of stuff.

Devotees dress in Victorian garb, favouring lumpy pocket watches, retro fountain pens and old leather gloves. They're still wedded to their smart phones and laptops of course, but they disguise them with leather and lace as Victorian artifacts. The mission statement seems to be "we embrace technology, but only early technology. We shop at thrift stores, thereby rejecting the rampant consumerism we see around us and heartily disapprove of."

If you've seen the movie *The League of Extraordinary Gentlemen* or either of Robert Downey, Jr.'s Sherlock Holmes epics you know how to dress Steampunk. Go for it. Godspeed, my friend.

Do I sound spiteful? I'm not. Just weary and confused at the loopy world I live in. I must have moaned or sighed out loud because my son, by way of making me feel better, said, "Steampunk's out now. It's all about Normcore."

Normcore? Normcore?? What the hell's (etcetera).

Normcore (my son tells me) is an even trendier form of fashion statement that is pretty much the polar opposite of Steampunk. The motif of Normcore is averageness.

The point being not to stop traffic like a morning glory but to blend in like a common, garden-variety weed. It is dressing to disappear rather than to stand out. Thus a Normcore aficionado might wear a bowling shirt, sweat pants and a baseball cap to a shopping mall.

Normcores don't wear high-end Nikes; they wear Crocs. They don't wear gear from Gap or Roots; they wear off-the-rack cheapos from Zellers or Kmart. It is no longer cool to try to look cool.

Quite a flip in my lifetime. I came of age in the tie-dyed, hippy-dippy, flower power, psychedelic bell-bottom, look-at-me world of the sixties and seventies. I never dressed like that—I'm a Canadian, for crying out loud— but I fantasized about it.

Nope, I guess I've always been a few city blocks behind the fashion curve. Except . . .

I stopped walking. I looked at my son. We were in a mall. I was wearing a baseball cap, cargo shorts, a T-shirt and flip-flops.

"Woo-hoo!" I crowed. "I'm a trendsetter."

My son rolled his eyes. But in a respectful way.

Curtains for Car Culture

The first thing an American does when he gets a little ahead, he buys an auto. Second thing he does is drive it over the horizon.
WALT ROSTOW, AMERICAN HAWK, CIRCA 1960

*G*ather 'round youngsters, and I'll spin you a yarn about a time when girls' skirts were short, men's hair was long and Detroit was Motown, where music—and the car—was king.

Especially the car. It sounds almost quaint now, but there was a time when the auto in the driveway was practically a member of the family, and not just in Detroit—all over North America. Back then a large chunk of our lives revolved around the car. We took Sunday drives as families. Young boys memorized the styles and models year by year. Tailfins waxed and waned. Even I could distinguish a Chevy Impala from a Pontiac Laurentian at 200 yards.

Autos ruled. We had drive-in movies and drive-thru restaurants and banks. The greatest sexual attractant an unattached male could dangle was His Own Car.

Young studs even installed small purple "sex lights" under the dash to emphasize our hotness.

Why did the automobile loom so large in our lives? Aside from hormones, I think it was the freedom cars promised. As a young and restless lout of the fifties and sixties I desperately wanted to escape the claustrophobic clutches of my home and my neighbourhood. How better to do that then as a knight of the road, breezily wheeling my steed (they weren't measured in horsepower for no reason) over two-laned hill and dale.

But then the two lanes became four, then eight—even sixteen. The air turned skanky and road rage ruled. Travel by car became less of an adventure, more of an ordeal. Trying to drive from A to B became more onerous than staying at home with mom and dad.

And of course there were fewer attractive places to go. We'd paved most of them and turned the rest into parking lots.

Throw in a recession or two, random gougings at the gas pump and skyrocketing insurance rates. It wasn't long before the bloom faded on the automotive rose. Kids don't worship cars or car ownership anymore. Since 2005 the number of miles driven annually by American 16- to 24-year-olds has dropped 23 percent.

For many reasons. Lots more of us live in cities than ever before and driving in cities is a large and expensive pain in the butt.

And then there's the Internet. We used to rely on cars to hang out with our friends, check out movies, socialize and meet new people. What we were really doing is moving our brains around. Today you can do all that on your smart phone, without getting out of your pyjamas.

Ralph Slovenko wrote 30 years ago: "Instead of bringing people together, the automobile tends to isolate them. Instead of walking or strolling or sitting outside, the American roams in his car, in his boxes, and he encounters other boxes, not people."

That's the sad part. We haven't outgrown cars; we've just replaced them with smaller boxes.

It's All Over, Cupcake

*H*ere's some breaking news—the cupcake is dead. Well, it is in New York anyway. Crumbs Bake Shop, one of the heavy hitters in the Gotham gourmet cupcake business, has seen the value of its shares plunge 34 percent to an all-time low. At one time it fetched $13 a share; last I checked you could pick one up for 27 cents.

I can't say I'm astonished. The cupcake craze had "passing fad à la hula hoop" written all over it from the time the first shops opened back in the early years of the millennium. Imagine: a phenomenon that owed its existence to a single episode of the TV soap opera *Sex and the City,* which happened to feature a cupcake shop. Talk about a flimsy foundation.

For the discerning observer cupcakes were always a mere flash in the baking pan. They never grew the commercial legs of, say, doughnuts.

The doughnut. Now there is a gustatory delectation you can take to the bank. Not only is the humble doughnut hale and hearty, it's spawning new and exotic offspring faster than a Kardashian collects grooms. The cupcake craze may be cratering in New York but doughnut hybrids are rising in the ashes. A Lower East Side enterprise called Doughnut Plant (motto: We Doan Need No Steenkin *Sex and the City*) is doing turn-away business offering items such as a number crested with roasted chestnuts and crème brûlée. They fly off the shelves as fast as they can bake them.

Meanwhile in Washington there's a joint called Zeke's DC Donutz that offers a blitz of blintzes that you'd never find at Tim Hortons. Exhibit A: a peanut butter frosted doughnut topped with a slice of undercooked bacon.

Which is tame stuff compared to what's on the menu at Glam Doll Donuts of Minneapolis. At Glam Doll, Goth-clad servers with stainless steel implants in locations you don't want to know about dish up pricey sliders with names like Femme Fatale, Bombshell and Chart Topper, which is described as an "unexpectedly perfect topping blend of peanut butter and sriracha."

Sriracha? Sounds like a skin disease.

Clearly there are some major mutations going on in the world of baked buns. Take McDonald's. The world-famous franchise is rolling out a new version of its Egg McMuffin that is, um, egg-free. Well, yolk-free anyway. It still features a whole-grain muffin, Canadian bacon and white cheese but the rest is only egg whites, which means the all-new "Egg White Delight" contains about 50 fewer calories than the regular Egg McMuffin.

You don't have to order the new version, by the way. The always popular, belly-busting Egg McMuffin is still on the menu.

But the most disheartening news on the snack front has to come from Wonton Food, a New York company that happens to manufacture most of the fortune cookies in the world.

And Wonton Food, alas, has been bitten by the political correctness bug.

It seems the company has been receiving complaints from consumers about the romantic messages found in their fortune cookies. You know. Messages like, "One who admires you greatly is hidden before your eyes."

Well, some consumers (clearly people without actual lives) have deemed such messages "offensive" and "sexist." Wonton Food is bowing to the public pressure and replacing such sentiments with treacly, Happy Face pronouncements like, "You make every day special."

Gag me with a wonton soup spoon.

Fingering the Snoops

*C*an I tell you about my career as a photojournalist?

Won't take long because it didn't last long—about 11 seconds, as I recall.

I had the equipment—a nice 35-mm Pentax. I had the location—a mountain village in rural Spain. I had a customer—*The Globe and Mail* was buying travel pieces from me. I even had the occasion. Generalissimo Francisco Franco had just croaked and I had a chance to record what the passing of the long-time dictator meant to at least some of his countrymen. I decided a photograph of one of the townspeople—a barefoot peasant in a battered straw hat who was astride a burro shambling down a rocky path toward me—would make a compelling illustration for my story. I raised my camera; the peasant raised his right forefinger and wagged it disapprovingly.

And I caved. I baled. I chickened out. I lowered my camera and grinned apologetically. Clearly I wasn't tough enough to be a photojournalist.

Back then attitudes toward photos taken without permission were a good deal crisper than they are today. In 2015 we all have our pictures taken by complete strangers dozens of times daily. Surveillance cameras snap our profiles in bank lineups, corner stores, at gas pumps—even at stoplights. It is a completely unwarranted and unsanctioned intrusion of our privacy but it happens so often we don't even think about it.

My computer guru was helping me retrieve some files on my laptop and I happened to mention that tiny Cyclopean eye that sits front and centre on most laptop screens—the camera lens. He chuckled and said, "I can't tell you how many clients I deal with who've put duct tape over that lens."

Meaning what? That some people think their own computers are spying on them? What would be the point? What would a spy see through that lens? In my case he'd see a bald guy with a red face saying bad words about the laptop that just ate his email.

Hard to see how that would enhance the CSIS database of terrorist activity in Canada.

I'm saying CSIS but choose your own initials? CSA, FBI, CIA, RCMP—who knows who's snooping out there?

Recently I attended an anti-oil tanker rally in a local park. I was having a hard time hearing the Raging Grannies because of a high-pitched droning sound from overhead. I looked up and saw . . . a drone, I guess. A weird gizmo about the size of a crow with four stiff wings that swept back and forth about 20 feet above the crowd. It wasn't camouflaged—as a matter of fact it looked sort of like a model airplane—except every few seconds it would stop and hover.

The better to take photographs, I have to conclude.

So, who was manning the controls on that drone? The protest organizers? Some municipal crowd control bureaucrat? A constable from the local RCMP unit?

All I know is, nobody identified themselves. And nobody asked my permission.

Well, I know something else. The next time I pass a surveillance camera—at the bank, at the gas pump, wherever—I plan to emulate that Spanish peasant who held up his forefinger to me years ago.

But I'll be using a different finger.

Look! Up in the Sky! It's . . .

*N*ot to alarm you or anything, but suppose tomorrow morning you looked over the rim of your Tim Hortons double-double to perceive a massive fireball screaming across the heavens toward you.

Suppose further that this fireball turned out to be an incoming meteor travelling at, let's call it, 67,600 kilometres an hour. And for the sake of argument, let's imagine the fireball exploded right over your town.

Already happened, my friend—February 2012. The resulting shock wave burst with what scientists say was the force of 40 Hiroshimas, shattering thousands of windows and injuring more than 1,600 people, who suffered everything from temporary blindness to skin-peeling sunburns. Thing is, it happened over the remote city of Chelyabinsk in Russia, so we hardly heard about it.

In any case this meteor was little more than a cosmic snowball, as meteors go—merely 19 metres in diameter. Scientists estimate there may be as many as 20 million space rocks that size whizzing around our solar system.

Up until the Chelyabinsk incident scientists didn't even bother tracking space junk that small. They figured only rocks more than 30 metres across were dangerous. Chelyabinsk has changed the odds. Scientists used to say we could expect a serious hit from outer space about once every century and a half; now they reckon it's more like once every 30 years.

We've seen this movie before. Back in 1908 a comet exploded over the Tunguska region of Russia, flattening an estimated 80 million trees and scaring the bejeebers out of thousands of rural Russians.

Then, of course, there was the Big One. Sixty-five million years ago an asteroid six miles wide ploughed into Mexico's Yucatan, unleashing worldwide tsunamis, forest fires, acid rain and—many believe—an eviction notice to the world's dinosaur population.

Canada's number has also come up in the meteor lottery. Eons ago an uninvited intruder from outer space scoured a crater 16 miles wide and 40 miles long creating Ontario's Sudbury Basin and leaving behind a vast and rich mineral deposit for which, nearly two billion years later, shareholders in Inco are still giving thanks.

Naturally, such an event had minimal effect on Sudbury's property values, occurring as it did back in the Paleoproterozoic era—but what if it happened today? And how likely is that anyway?

More likely than we'd like to think and more likely than we used to believe. According to the journal *Science*, the experts now reckon the Earth is seven times more likely to get seriously stoned from outer space than was previously believed—and they're talking about rocks even bigger than the one that exploded over Chelyabinsk a few years back.

And don't forget: that one exploded in the atmosphere. What if it had ploughed into the city? Or into New York? Or Toronto? Or Salt Spring Island?

Not to alarm you or anything.

If You Knew Sushi . . .

In Mexico we have a word for sushi. Bait.

JOSÉ SIMON

Reactionary as it may sound, I feel a touch of empathy for Señor Simon. I, too, tend to avoid sushi. Generally speaking I prefer the concept of cooked food over raw—especially food that may contain unwelcome surprises such as anisakiasis. This is an infection of the gut caused by little wrigglers known as *Anisakis* larvae. They normally live in fish guts but are happy to move uptown to take up residence in yours.

You don't want *Anisakis* larvae in your alimentary neighbourhood. They're painful, unpleasant and hard to get rid of. Granted, the chances of ingesting *Anisakis* larvae in sushi, sashimi, ceviche or other raw fish dishes are remote, but cooking the fish reduces the risk to zero. Ergo, fire up the burners, ma.

But then what is one to make of the fact that there's an upscale Tokyo restaurant called Ne Quitez Pas where clients line up to taste the latest culinary creations of famed chef Toshio Tanabe? Maestro Tanabe specializes in dishes featuring, well, dirt. Diners can sample the delights of soil soup, which is served with a flake of dirty truffle and, for the truly adventurous, there's the "Soil Surprise," a dirt-encrusted potato that features an unwashed truffle centre.

What separates chef Tanabe from a kindergartner in a sandbox? Hey, it's not like he serves raw dirt—he simmers it slightly after running it through a sieve to get rid of crunchy bits.

When it comes to restaurant food, occasionally life imitates art—or at least the human digestive system. Take the case of the McDonald's outlet in the city of Dorval, Quebec. The restaurant is being sued for . . . clogging arteries.

Not human arteries—municipal ones. Dorval city fathers claim that discarded grease from the McDonald's galley has bunged up city sewers resulting in nearly $15,000 worth of damage.

Perhaps they could cram an industrial-strength antacid tablet down the galley drainpipe.

Different strokes. There's a man-and-wife couple in Gibsons, BC, transforming the very concept of breakfast with a cereal they've created that's chock-full of organic goodies. It's name is . . . well, the name originally was Hapi until one of their first customers tasted a spoonful and yelped, "Holy crap! This is amazing!"

Holy Crap it was. It's a breakfast sensation now sold all over Canada and in 40 other countries. It also made it to the International Space Station where Chris Hadfield and colleagues chowed down on Holy Crap for breakfast as they looped around the earth.

Think of that—a humble cereal concoction conceived by a couple of Canucks in a small town in British Columbia orbiting the heavens in the bellies of astronauts.

Holy crap indeed.

Scooting Hither and Yon

*A*nother glorious summer is unfolding its wings here in the lower left-hand corner of our great nation, accompanied, it must be said, by those swooping, buzzing, whining harbingers of warmer weather.

No, not gnats and mosquitos. I'm talking about Vespas and Vinos and Zumas and Ruckuses. I'm talking about motor scooters, that intermediate step between golf carts and motorcycles. A step that more and more West Coasters seem to be stepping up to.

I hate to sound like a smart aleck, but what took us so long? Much of the rest of the world figured out the scooter advantage decades ago. The streets of Spain, France and Italy are owned by motor scooters. In the city of Saigon alone there are six million registered motor scooters.

Why? Because scooters make sense. Not on the highway, perhaps, but 90 percent of the trips we make don't involve highway driving, and scooters can easily keep up with urban traffic. As for parking, you can stow three scooters in the space taken up by one car.

Better than a motorcycle? Unless you've got a James Dean complex, yeah. Much cheaper, for starters. And with plenty of horsepower to get you around our towns and cities. You don't even need a motorcycle licence.

Oh, and gas. You've noticed how the price of gas soars and dips? I heard an oil company executive explain on the radio that the price of gas always goes up in the summer because people drive more in the summer. In any other business that would be called extortion, but that's another rant. My point is, if you ride a scooter you don't much care when the price of gas goes up a few cents a litre because you can fill your tank and drive for a week on way less than ten bucks anyway.

Disadvantages? Smirks from passing Marlon Brando wannabes and it is tough to take your sheep dog to the vet's on a scooter. Also, I wouldn't want to try cramming a week's worth of groceries in the itsy-bitsy scooter trunk. Plus snowy, icy roads are a non-starter—but how many snow days did you suffer through last winter? So when it's inconvenient you take the car or call a cab or hitch a ride with a car-driving friend. And all the other times? Take your scooter. Think of all the Greenie points you'll rack up.

Mind you, if you take advantage of it in the summer months, be warned. You'll have to put up with those swooping, buzzing, whining harbingers that come out at this time of year.

No, not scooters. Gnats and mosquitoes. You'll ride through swarms of them from time to time. So if you do ride a scooter, be sure to wear goggles or sunglasses. And unless you want to pick bugs out of your teeth, don't grin.

Even though you'll want to.

Everything New is Old Again

The pimply-faced kid in the backwards-facing ball cap shows up to fix my laptop, taps a couple of keys, shrugs and says, "It's dead. You probably need to replace it."

Yes, of course. It's almost six years old. A total fossil.

This is my fourth—or is it fifth—personal computer. It's the latest in a daisy chain of technological bewilderment and woe that stretches all the way back to an ancient clunky Commodore 64, which is the machine that first seduced me away from my old Olivetti typewriter.

The one that never broke down, never crashed, never lost a file and never once in 30 years required the ministrations of a typewriter expert. This despite gallons of spilled coffee on its keyboard, breadcrumbs and cigar ashes in its innards, frequent manual abuse and once, being hurled right off my desk into a wall (impending deadline; writer's block). I never thought much about my old Olivetti when I had it but in retrospect I mourn for it like a lost love. I miss its music: the ta-pocketa peck of the keys striking the paper; the ka-ching of the bell that warned me I was nearing the end of a line; the *whirr* and *ka-boom* of the carriage as I cuffed it across to start a new line.

Oh hell. If you're under 40 reading this I might as well explain how to harpoon a whale. You have no idea what I'm talking about.

Used to be you couldn't find an office without at least one typewriter. Now they've vanished into the landfill of history, along with Eaton's catalogues, fax machines, garter belts and buggy whips.

And public telephones. Pay phones haven't disappeared entirely, but as an urban feature that used to be on every street corner they are now as scarce as flamingos. That's not a surprise given that just about everyone nowadays totes a plastic lozenge that can make calls, take calls and tell you the current humidity reading in Mogadishu.

Humans now carry more information in their breast pocket or purse than our grandparents would access in a lifetime. The fact that the majority use it to play Angry Birds or tweet a review of our latest purchase at Tim Hortons? The fault, dear Brutus, is not in our stars.

Or in our BlackBerrys.

There is a brand new hotel in the city of Victoria—or rather a brand new "old" hotel—called Hotel Zed. Sixty-two rooms all retrofitted to whisk the client right back to, oh, say 1967. The colour scheme is sixties-psychedelic, there's a Ping-Pong table in the lobby along with, yes, actual typewriters that guests can use. Each room has a bulletin board instead of a guest directory, old-fashioned alarm clocks, radios you can actually see the dial on . . .

And telephones.

Real telephones. The clunky Bakelite ones with the curly cords and the one ringy-dingy, two ringy-dingy rotary dial right in the middle. You'll find the rotary phone right by the bed in your room at the Hotel Zed.

And if you're a little mystified by the device, not to worry. There's a How-to-Use-It guide in the drawer. Or you could just hold your iPhone up to the phone and click. You'll get an instruction video.

Not sure how to use a rotary phone? Hey, there's an app for that.

Part 6

THE GOOD, THE BAD
AND THE JUST PLAIN WEIRD

Trophy Hunting: Too Much to Bear

I have no quarrel with hunters. As a matter of fact I admire the man or woman who goes out and harvests his or her own protein. Such people are less hypocritical than, oh, say, me. I harvest my protein from the local supermarket, letting someone else do the dirty work of shifting said protein from the forest or the feedlot to my dinner plate.

I respect subsistence hunters but trophy hunters, people who hunt just for the thrill of killing something big?

You suck.

I'm thinking specifically of one Clayton Stoner, a BC boy who recently had his picture taken holding up the severed head of a grizzly he shot on the BC coast near Bella Bella. Mr. Stoner wasn't interested in the body of the bear—he left that to rot on the forest floor. He just wanted the bragging rights to the head.

Must have been real tough to shoot the grizzly, which was known as "Cheeky" to the folks who knew him. I imagine Cheeky was shambling toward Mr. Stoner looking for a handout about the time the heavy calibre bullets smashed into his chest. Or maybe he was just standing on his hind legs sniffing the wind and wondering what the odd creature in camouflage clothes squinting down a shiny stick was doing in his neighbourhood.

Oh well, it's not as if Mr. Stoner is singular in any way, or breaking the law, come to that. Killing grizzlies is big business in British Columbia. The province sells killing rights in two trophy hunts every year. Between 2001 and 2011 nearly 3,000 grizzlies—900 of them females—were "legally" slaughtered by trophy hunters.

Is this a popularly supported money-maker for the government? Hardly. First Nations oppose it, environmentalists decry it and 80 percent of all British Columbians want it stopped.

Especially since the government handles it so ineptly. Each year the number of kills exceeds the limits set by bear management policy. There are only about 15,000 grizzlies in the entire province. By sanctioning the slaughter of more than 300 prime animals a year we're cutting it fine. According to biologist Kyle Artelle, grizzlies "have great difficulties recovering from population declines. A sow may have a litter of three young every three years."

What's even scarier: we only *think* there are 15,000 grizzlies left. It's a government estimate—from the same geniuses who ran the east coast cod fishery into extinction.

It's a dangerous game to play, risking the future of a magnificent species just to satisfy the fantasies of men suffering from the twin afflictions of too much money and penile inadequacy. If we must have blood money, how about a trophy hunting season on . . . trophy hunters?

I'm sure even Darwin would approve.

James (Bottled in) Bond

*A*re you old enough to remember when boozing was cool? When the airwaves foamed over with cheery beer ads and Christmas season magazines featured full-colour depictions of Santa relaxing after a hard night's work with a noggin of Captain Morgan at his elbow?

I can remember when "drink up, boys" was what everyone did just before they picked up their car keys and drove home; when the guy at the office party wearing a lampshade and propositioning the receptionist was regarded as amusing, not pathetic and repulsive. I remember the days when most of us thought alcohol was a good buddy and a swell social enabler, not a treacherous weasel out to embarrass and possibly kill us. And I remember the international icon who exemplified elegant boozing in all its glory—James Bond. Sophisticated, unflappable James Bond, ordering—in between offing baddies and boffing beauties—his martinis "shaken, not stirred." Turns out that Mr. Bond wasn't so cool. He had a bigger problem than SMERSH, STDs or the wrath of M.

Turns out 007 was a lush.

That's not my conclusion. You'll find it in the pages of the *British Medical Journal*. Researchers for the magazine analyzed all of the Bond books written by his creator, Sir Ian Fleming, ferreting out the hero's alcohol intake. They noted every martini, highball, flute of champagne, glass of wine and bottle of beer. They conservatively factored in every vague reference—when Bond "called for the drink tray," "got drunk" or "had drinks"— and concluded that Bond's famous "licence to kill" was aimed primarily at his own liver. Of the 123.5 days that are chronicled, Bond abstained on only 48.5 of them—and 36 of those dry days weren't by choice. Bond was either in the slammer, recovering in hospital or otherwise constrained from reaching a bottle.

The researchers further reckon that, on average, Bond was downing about 75 grams of pure alcohol every day—more than twice the danger level set out by Bond's own British National Health Service.

He was also susceptible to bouts of Rob Fordian excess. On the third day of Bond's adventures in *From Russia with Love*, researchers extrapolate that the secret agent chugged the equivalent of nearly 400 grams of pure alcohol. That's like 14 vodka martinis or 25 beers. You try aiming a Walther PPK after a dozen or so martinis.

Or aiming anything else, come to that. The *British Medical Journal* study notes that Bond's intake would have him flirting with hypertension, stroke, depression and, ahem, extreme sexual dysfunction.

Meanwhile, an article in another medical magazine, the *International Journal of Clinical Medicine*, chronicles the case of an unnamed 61-year-old Texan who was recently hospitalized for "extreme inebriation." Trouble is, he denied having a single drink. A medical examination revealed that he was telling the truth. The man suffers from a condition known as auto-brewery syndrome. Simply put, his stomach makes beer. His gut contains yeast that converts all starches (even vegetables and grains) into ethanol. The man can get a buzz from downing a Big Mac.

If James Bond existed, he'd be eating his heart out.

Having already dispatched his liver.

A-Hunting We Won't Go

*T*he world's oldest living animal is dead.

Was murdered, actually, but I'll get to that.

Geezer organisms aren't that rare, really. We've known lots of venerable critters that achieved a ripe vintage. A house cat in Texas made it to the age of 38; a horse named Ol' Billy in London popped off at 62; a tortoise in India still waddles along at 255 years of age.

But that's just a short recess compared to the record established by our lately departed. Ming was 507 years old. Not bad.

For a clam.

An Icelandic clam, to be precise. It was dredged up by scientists on a research vessel from the Bangor School of Ocean Science off the northern coast of Iceland. Scientists could tell the clam was pretty old but they couldn't tell exactly how old.

So they killed it and carbon dated the corpse. Turned out he was just a little over five centuries old. The scientists named him Ming because he dated from the same period as the Ming Dynasty in China. As the song says, we always hurt the ones we love. Ask the dodo, the passenger pigeon, the east coast cod or the horizon-to-horizon herds of bison that used to populate the plains.

Those extirpations were caused by simple, stupid, human

greed but we're not above species slaughter in the name of science. Take John James Audubon. Now there was an environmentalist, right? The nineteenth-century ornithologist-cum-painter took it upon himself to document, on canvas, every North American bird he could find. Did a fine job too. His magnificent *Birds of America* contains full-colour illustrations from more than 435 paintings of more than 700 bird species. Audubon even discovered 25 species of birds never before documented. He made extensive notes and meticulous paintings of each and every bird. Right after he shot them.

Audubon shot and killed every bird he ever painted—and more. Sometimes he blew dozens out of the sky or off a branch before he found what he considered to be a perfect specimen.

The man loved his work. On one outing he recorded that he shot 30 partridges, 27 grey squirrels, a woodcock, a barn owl, a turkey buzzard and one yellow warbler. Lucky for Ming and his clammy compatriots that Audubon wasn't into molluscs.

Oscar Wilde dismissed fox hunting as the unspeakable in pursuit of the inedible. Call me pussified, but the charm of tracking down unthreatening critters to put bullets in them continues to elude me.

Still love a good hunting story, though. Like the one about two hunters—let's call them Larry and Moe—who are crossing a pasture when a pheasant explodes into flight right between them. Larry fires and misses; Moe fires and hits Larry. Moe frantically dials 9-1-1 on his cellphone. "Help!" he squawks. "I've shot my pal Larry! I think I might have killed him!"

"Calm down," says the emergency response dispatcher. "First, we need to find out if he's dead."

The dispatcher hears a moment of silence followed by the sound of a gunshot. Moe comes back on the line.

"Okay, he's dead. Now what?"

Read This, If You Would Be So Kind

Mike Defazio is pulling into his autobody shop in Saint John, NB, when KA-BAM!—he hits a pothole the size of Mike Duffy's belly imprint and blows a tire. "Enough is enough," says Defazio. He proceeds to patch the offending pothole. "I spent three and a half hours," says Mike, "I filled numerous potholes. Some of them were twelve inches wide, a foot deep and two feet long." Big mistake.

Mr. Defazio received a visit from the Saint John Department of Transportation and Environment Services. They told him that he had violated a city bylaw. They said a city works crew would be sent out to undo the work he had done and they would send him a bill for it.

Mr. Defazio said various unprintable things but faced with legal action he softened and agreed to undo his own work. "I told him everything, all the rocks, all the potholes, could go back to the way it was, and he said, 'That's what we want.'"

So Mr. Defazio hired a local contractor and $450 later, drivers can once again blow a tire pulling into Mr. Defazio's autobody shop.

I hate to come on like some cracker-barrel philosopher, but we seem to have a problem with simple generosity these days. There was a time when we all just kind of looked out for one another, no questions asked. Cut the old fella's grass next door, shovelled out the driveway for the widow woman on the corner, did some shopping for the veteran with arthritis.

Now we hesitate because there are "liability issues" to consider.

Sometimes we don't just hesitate. We call the cops.

Happened to Richard Wright in Halifax. He was going around handing out hundred-dollar bills to total strangers. The Mounties shipped him off to a mental-health facility for a "wellness check."

But what if there was nothing wrong with Richard Wright? What if he was perfectly healthy, utterly sane and just feeling generous?

Turns out that was the case—as the Mounties would have learned had they contacted his family before they shipped him off to the funny farm. His daughter Chelsea told a newspaper reporter that her dad "worked hard for his money, had no mental-health issues and simply wants to help people." A close friend described Wright as "a generous individual wrapped up in acts of kindness."

Acts of kindness. What a subversive notion.

Which brings us to the other side of the country—to a man named Brice Royer. Two years ago Mr. Royer discovered he had stomach cancer. He wondered if it was caused by the high-pressure life style he lived. So he moved from Vancouver to bucolic Deep Cove. He started eating a healthy diet, listening to the trees. And he discovered a concept called Pay It Forward. Simply put, it's a philosophy followed by communities and some businesses around the world in which people give away stuff, expecting nothing in return. They give everything—services, instruction, accommodation, even washing machines and automobiles. The bottom line with Pay It Forward is the idea that money transactions separate people, whereas giving things for nothing creates trust and forges real communities.

Recently somebody gave Brice Royer a minivan. No charge. The giver thought the gesture would help him teach the concept of generosity to his six-year-old son.

Potholes in Saint John, hundred-dollar bills in Halifax, a minivan in Deep Cove. Two steps back, but one step forward.

It's a Conspiracy!

I know somebody who thinks humans can defy gravity.

Really. She believes it's possible for people to float up out of their loafers and bump around the room like a guppy in an aquarium. Weird thing is, she's no dingbat in a tinfoil hat. She's a journalist, a university graduate and seemingly a rational, sentient human.

She just thinks Newton and that law of gravity stuff is bull crap.

I met her at a party over the chip dip. In a perfect world I would have crosschecked her with a crisp, no-nonsense, Christopher Hitchens-style broadside. Instead I said something incisive like, "Could you pass the nachos?" I've never been effective dealing with the gullible and paranoid. They leave me tongue-tied and creeped out.

And they're everywhere. I've met people who believe the earth was created in six days, others who are certain there's a flying saucer quarantined in Roswell. Some insist the moon landing was play-acted on a desert in Nevada, others that the Canadian government is poisoning us all with chemicals dropped from unmarked airplanes.

Modern Russia (an oxymoron) is a cornucopia of crackpots

these days, which is not surprising. Gullibility and paranoia thrive when you have a captive press that broadcasts whatever the government dictates. Thus the Russian populace has been assured by state-run TV that Malaysia Airlines flight 17 (which virtually all non-Russian experts agree was shot down by a Russian-supplied missile) was actually loaded with week-old corpses before it took off and then detonated over Ukraine to frame pro-Russian forces.

In the winter of 2013 a massive explosion over the town of Chelyabinsk injured nearly a thousand Russians and destroyed buildings. Scientists determined it was caused by a meteor strike. Shockingly large numbers of Russians still believe it was caused by Americans testing a new super weapon.

Not that the Russians have a corner on the nutbar market. (Elvis? Is that you?) There are still, incredibly, people who believe that Elvis Presley didn't die on his bathroom floor nearly 40 years ago.

The Elvis deniers prefer to believe that the Legend became an undercover agent for the Drug Enforcement Agency; that he's in the Witness Protection Program; that he was abducted by aliens; that he faked his death and is presently living in a secret seven-storey underground condo beneath Graceland along with Michael Jackson, who also faked his death.

But that's not my favourite. My favourite is the theory that the British Royal Family, along with the Bushes and the Clintons, are not really humans at all. They are actually man-eating, shape shifting, lizard-people from the fourth dimension.

Ridiculous. Now Stephen Harper, I could believe . . .

When it comes to gullibility and paranoia, George Carlin said it best: "Tell people there's an invisible man in the sky who created the universe and the vast majority will believe you. Tell them the paint is wet, and they have to touch it to be sure."

Of course George Carlin didn't really die. He's playing drums underground at Graceland in a trio with Elvis and Mikey.

Where Have All the Heroes Gone?

*A*uthorities in Nepal will install a ladder to provide a shortcut over a steep cliff near the peak of Mount Everest. A government spokesman said the ladder would "ease congestion" for climbers on their way to the summit.

Hm. As a guy with exactly zero aspirations to climb the world's highest mountain (or indeed anything higher than that brick of mango ice cream at the back of the freezer), excuse me for asking but isn't the whole point of climbing Mount Everest the fact that there are no ladders?

Isn't climbing Mount Everest supposed to be hard? And dangerous? And uncomfortable? If not, why not install a series of heated escalators from base camp? Why not hot air balloons with celebrity hosts? (Kim Kardashian does Kathmandu!)

Edmund Hillary and Tenzing Norgay ascended Everest 60 years ago wearing wool and leather. They wouldn't recognize the be-Spandexed, Rolexed and oxygen-bottled tourists who ascend the peak in catered droves these days. Modern-day Everest wannabes aren't so much brave and hardy; more rich and bored.

Why do we make it so difficult to be heroic anymore?

In some quarters "hero" has become a dirty word. At a Pennsylvania preschool "super hero play" and "monster games" have been banned because school authorities fear they make kids "dangerously overactive." One child came home and told his mother that "make-believe isn't allowed at school anymore."

Closer to home, there's the case of Briar McDonnell. Briar's a Grade 7 student in Calgary who saw a kid being harassed by another student. The boy was being taunted, pushed and prodded.

And then there was the knife. Briar didn't see it, but his classmates did and Briar "heard the flick." Nevertheless, Briar stepped in and pushed the bully away. A teacher intervened, the principal was called and . . .

Briar was commended, right? Congratulated? Singled out at assembly as a good guy? Given honourable mention in the school yearbook?

Nah. He was hauled down to the principal's office and treated like a criminal. The police were summoned and Briar's locker was searched. His mother was called and told that her son had been "involved in an incident" in which he "decided to play hero and jumped in."

"We don't condone heroics," the principal harrumphed. Briar, she explained, should have gone off and found a teacher to handle the situation.

Briar's mother wondered if, perhaps, in the time it would have taken Briar to find a teacher, the victim's throat might have been slit. The principal said that was "beside the point."

Mrs. McDonnell didn't agree.

"What are they teaching them?" she asked a *National Post* reporter. "That when you go out in the workforce and someone's not nice to you, you have to tattle to your boss? What are we going to do if there are no heroes in the world? There would be no police, no fire, no armed forces. . . ."

And probably no more people like Yuichiro Miura. The Japanese climber reached the peak of Mount Everest in May 2013, becoming the oldest person to do so. Mr. Miura is 80 years old.

He didn't need a ladder.

Want to Be a Crook? Think Big

Chances are you'll take a Mexican vacation next fall.

Chances are you'll find yourself on a sandy beach overlooking the gulf, slurping back a margarita as you work on your tan.

Chances are you'll notice a pudgy guy in sunglasses and Bermuda shorts doing the same thing in a chaise lounge next to you.

Chances are that'll be Ian Thow.

You remember him—the guy who as an "investment adviser" in Victoria bilked at least 20 clients, senior citizens, mostly, out of their life savings—$8 million that we know about—while he lived high on the hog in a five-star condo with a private plane at his disposal, enjoying all the perks that go with having millions of other people's dollars in your pocket.

Yeah, well. The Canadian justice system caught up with Mr. Thow and came down on him with both boots. He was tried, convicted and sentenced to nine years in the slammer back in 2010.

Less than three years later the Parole Board of Canada decided that Mr. Thow had suffered enough. The board okayed a one-week Mexican vacation for Mr. Thow.

But he'd be watched by guards, right? The Mexican constabulary would keep him under tabs? He'd wear an ankle monitor at least?

Nah. That would be too . . . intrusive. A spokesman for the board noted that Mr. Thow "has made a commitment to living pro-socially."

Whatever that means.

As for the possibility that after his fun in the sun Thow might just have decided to, you know, not board the Air Canada flight back home? "The Correctional Services and the parole officer are of the opinion that that is not a likelihood."

Ah, well. That's all right then.

Besides, it's not as if Thow would be a fish-belly white refugee from solitary confinement blinking in the Mexican sun. He's been cruising around the streets of Vancouver unsupervised since 2012, less than two years after his conviction. Doing what, exactly? The Parole Board "has no information available" on that.

Thow is small potatoes compared to Earl Jones, the Montreal ex-financial advisor who scammed $50 million from more than 1,500 clients, including friends, relatives and an 84-year-old widow named Joey Davis, who Jones took for $200,000. Jones was sentenced to 11 years in jail in 2010. He was released from prison on his own recognizance less than three years later.

Then there's the case of William Footman, a 55-year-old bank robber who was finally captured earlier this year. Footman was a busy thief. He hit 37 banks in New York before they finally took him down.

Mind you he didn't exactly rob the banks. He didn't take any money at all. He swiped their front door mats. "I sell them to bodegas," explained Footman. "Their floors get wet."

Mr. Footman is awaiting sentencing as I write.

Betcha he does more time than Ian Thow and Earl Jones combined.

The New F-Word: Fame

Of all the creepy things I know about Kim Kardashian (and they are legion) the creepiest is that she has fans. The Hollywood figure who's famous for, well, nothing, actually—she can't sing, dance, act, paint or string together enough platitudes to get invited on a talk show—is now flogging something called Kim Kardashian: Hollywood.

It's an online game that the gullible may download. The app shows you how to create your very own avatar that pretends to be Hollywood-bound in search of stardom. Not as an actor or a dancer or anything, you know, talented. Just as a celebrity, famous for being famous. Much like you-know-who. Your avatar will go to photo shoots for which virtual wardrobes must be purchased. Your avatar will get weary, for which energy boosts (Colombian marching powder, anyone?) need to be paid for. How to pay? Just head to the online Star Shop and purchase as many stars as you like. You can get 50 for $4.99. Or the Best Value Bargain: 1,250 stars for $99.99. Then you spend your stars to get your avatar up and running.

The app is free to download and the perks are imaginary but the money spent to obtain them is very real. Star-struck kids have spent hundreds of dollars apiece helping their avatars pursue fame. Experts predict Kim Kardashian: Hollywood will gross $200 million in its first year.

A visiting Martian might be forgiven for asking: What's going on?

Good question. Whatever it is, it was also going on at the Toronto International Film Festival last fall. TIFF is a big deal. It attracts world-class films and the people who produce, direct and star in them. People like David Cronenberg, Atom Egoyan, Kate Winslet, Al Pacino . . .

And Justin Bieber.

What? Bieber??? The teenybopper princeling of high school hooliganism and over-refreshed dumb-ass misdemeanours? What's that mutt doing at a film festival?

Doesn't matter. He was there and the TV cameras and the Hollywood paparazzi followed him around like a flock of seagulls tracking a shrimp boat. The actor John Cusack, also at TIFF, was totally mystified at the Bieber TV coverage.

"They had, like a Wolf Blitzer Situation Room," Cusack said. "They'd go to a reporter on location saying, 'He's been on this street,' and 'Here he is in a mall,' and 'Here we see him kissing his girlfriend.'"

Cusack was nonplussed. "This is a film festival," Cusack said. "It's awesome that the guy actually likes films, but . . ."

Exactly. But who cares?

Millions, apparently. When it comes to lowest common denominator media pandering, nothing can be too trivial.

Neil Postman, in *Amusing Ourselves to Death: Public Discourse in the Age of Show Business*, once compared the visionaries George Orwell, who wrote *1984*, and Aldous Huxley, who wrote *Brave New World*, thus:

"Orwell feared those who would ban books. Huxley feared there would be no reason to ban books because no one would want to read one . . . Orwell feared the truth would be concealed from us. Huxley feared that the truth would be drowned in a sea of irrelevance."

What-evvvver!

Who needs to read a book when you can "like" the Biebs on Facebook or channel Kim K on your iPhone?

I mean, like, Hel-LO!

A Big Hand for the Little People

*L*enin was a half-pint. So were Stalin and Hitler. Genghis Khan? A shrimp for all his bloodthirstiness—no more than five foot one. The French artist Toulouse Lautrec didn't even make the five-foot mark, which is why Parisian courtesans called him "our little teapot."

Well, one reason.

There are lots of famous people who never could have made the basketball team. Dolly Parton's only five feet tall and Danny de Vito's not even that. Then there's the baseball player Eddie Gaedel, who played for the St. Louis Browns back in the 1950s. Truth to tell, Eddie was no great shakes as a baseball player, but he was hell to pitch to. He was three foot seven inches tall.

I have a soft spot for little people, probably because I was a bit of a runt myself until puberty kicked in. I remember too well what it felt like to be picked last for the football team, answer to names like Shorty and Midget and to only come up to the mid-torso line of kids my age (although close dancing could be heavenly).

Mostly, though, it's not much fun being a Little Person in our macho culture, so it's comforting to know that in other locales being short isn't a handicap, it's a total asset. Germany, for instance, is a great place to be short. Especially if you're also a duck.

A German writer named Erica Fuchs has single-handedly created a whole intellectual subculture founded on, well, Donald Duck.

Really. She created an imaginary literary world in which Donald is a feathered philosopher, quoting Nietzsche and Kierkegaard. Uncle Scrooge has been re-christened Dagoberto and the kid nephews—Huey, Dewey and Louie—have been re-dubbed Tick, Trick and Track.

Sounds whacky (or quacky) but last year in Stuttgart academics from all over Germany convened for the 32nd annual convention of something billed as the German Organization for Non-Commercial Followers of Pure Donaldism.

Plenty of respect for small fry in Iceland, too, as the industrial giant Alcoa Inc. discovered when a company spokesman announced plans to build an aluminum smelter there.

Not so fast, the Icelandic government told the company. What sort of provision has been made for the protection of the Huldufólk?

"What's a Huldufólk?" the Alcoa reps asked.

Icelandic elves. In the end it took another six months of negotiations before the Icelandic authorities decided that the Huldufólk had been mollified and construction could go ahead.

Legend has it that the Huldufólk live under the surface rocks of Iceland and are fiercely protective of their homesteads. Some Icelanders build tiny homes in their gardens for the Huldufólk. They have ceremonial bonfires and leave out treats for them on Christmas Eve. Do all Icelanders believe in the Little People? A survey found that about 10 percent emphatically do. Another 10 percent do not.

The other 80 percent aren't saying.

Even the Icelandic pop star Björk is equivocal about the Huldufólk. "We believe Nature is stronger than Man," she says.

I'm down with that. Hats off to the Huldufólk, I say—and a doff of the homburg to all those fervent Donaldists in Germany.

At least the Donald they venerate is a duck, not a Trump.

Loving Our Treasures to Death

*A*re you up for a visit to Choquequirao? Probably not. It's hard to pronounce and even harder to get to. Choquequirao is nothing but ruins now, but five or six centuries ago it was a fabulous mountaintop refuge for Incan royalty. They called it the Cradle of Gold.

It was, and is, an exclusive destination. To get there nowadays you have to fly into Cuzco in Peru, and then drive for four hours on potholed, hairpin-turn mountain roads (watch for flash floods). Following that it's a brisk twelve- to sixteen-hour scramble along an often-terrifying mountain trail—and you're there.

But all that is about to change. The Peruvian government has approved construction of an aerial tramway that will span a deep canyon, connecting the ruined city with a highway that is only 15 minutes away. They reckon when the tramway's complete Choquequirao will be able to host 400 visitors an hour.

I have two words of advice for the Peruvian government: Please don't. I've seen this movie and it doesn't end well.

I've been to Venice.

The City of Bridges, AKA City of Light, City of Water has also been around for six centuries. Its founders also thought they could insulate it from the rest of the world, not by going to the top of a mountain but by choosing a location surrounded by water. Didn't work. As a matter of fact it's water access that has doomed that most beautiful of cities. Because it is accessible from the ocean, monster passenger ferries and giant cruise ships can sail right up to the city limits and disgorge their cargo—human rubberneckers from around the world. Sixty thousand tourists invade Venice every single day, unleashing an entire urban populace on the narrow medieval streets and lagoons every 24 hours.

Visiting Venice is not the soul-stirring spiritual experience it ought to be. It's more like going to Disneyland on Discount Saturday. Obnoxious Russians jostle with boorish Brits; tour leaders with amplified megaphones bray commentaries in French, Spanish and Italian. Children whine, flashing cellphones wave at the end of arms like clumsy daisies. Sweating hordes in plaid shorts and T-shirts mosey and meander and jostle disconsolately.

Funny how we do that. We love things to death. We poke and prod and tweak and facelift until whatever it was that attracted us is smothered, bloated and unrecognizable.

Not far from Venice another exercise in historical revisionism is unfolding. Italian archaeologists in Florence are picking over some mouldering bones in Florence's Santissima Annunziata Basilica. They're looking for the skeletal remains of a little boy, the son of Lisa Gherardini.

You know the mother better as Mona Lisa, the subject of Leonardo da Vinci's most famous portrait. The archaeologists think that they already have her bones from an earlier grave robbing. They're seeking a DNA match to confirm the identity.

Silvano Vinceti, a burlesque art huckster heading the team of . . . sorry, I don't know the Italian word for ghouls . . . says that if the DNA match is confirmed the project will move on into "it's most exciting phase—the reconstruction of Mona Lisa's face."

Scusi, signor, but that's already been done. Perfectly. By a chap named da Vinci.

Why don't you go down to Rome and play in the traffic?

Part 7

DUDE, WHERE'S MY COUNTRY?

Your Call Is Important to Us

Bureaucracy: Where they shoot the bull, pass the buck and make seven copies of everything.

E.C. McKENZIE

*F*or me, Toronto's City Hall is one of the most stunning edifices in the world.

Not because it's beautiful (although it is) but because it so perfectly marries form and function. You're familiar with the building? The hall itself, where politicians meet and policy is hammered out, looks like a hovering flying saucer, graceful and svelte. It is bracketed by two high-rise, silo-like towers full of offices. Years ago some anonymous wag summarized it perfectly: "The pearl of democracy surrounded by the oyster shell of bureaucracy."

Ah, bureaucracy. What is it in human nature that compels us to grow this cancerous carapace of delay, resistance, complication and rigidity around our best intentions? Bureaucracy is not just an infection exclusive to democracy. Totalitarian states are even worse. Think of communist Russia. Think North Korea.

A friend of mine says she can tell how hidebound a firm or institution is by making one phone call. "If the person who answers the phone can't help you," she says, "you know you're dealing with a bureaucracy."

So what about companies that greet you with an outright lie?

I'm talking about phone inquiries that are greeted by a recording that croons, "Your call is important to us."

No. No, it's not. If my call were important to you, you would provide gainful employment to a human being who could actually interact with me, rather than a preprogrammed HAL-like robot.

But that's what bureaucracy does. The truly sinister thing about bureaucracy is, it really is a cancer, feeding on and eventually destroying the host it supposedly serves. The writer Robert Conquest says: "The behaviour of any bureaucratic institution can best be understood by assuming it is controlled by a cabal of its enemies."

Think BlackBerry. Think Goldman Sachs.

Or if you really want to be creeped out, think the much-vaunted US Department of Homeland Security.

The 9/11 terrorist attacks were a supreme embarrassment to American security establishment. They'd been caught flat-footed by a gang of fanatical amateurs armed only with box cutters. One of the main recommendations following the attack: all emergency and rescue personnel needed to have one secure radio frequency merged into the Department of Homeland Security for ease of communication.

Uh-huh. So, a decade-plus later how's that working out?

Well, after an outlay of $430 million to build and operate that frequency, an internal survey reveals that out of 479 workers surveyed only one knew how to find the frequency, 72 percent of the staff didn't know it existed and 50 percent of the department's radios couldn't have accessed the frequency even if the employees knew where to look.

The Inspector General of the Department of Homeland Security admitted that if anything, the US might be more ill-equipped to deal with a terrorist attack than it was pre-9/11.

Something to think about the next time a voice on your phone tells you, "Your call is important to us."

Some Things You Auto Know

` Cars are our cathedrals.

ROLAND BARTHES

*H*olly Chabowski would certainly buy that premise. She's a British tourist who travelled across Canada with her Danish girlfriend in the summer of 2014. She was so moved by the experience she wrote an open letter to all of us. The letter was published in the *Ottawa Citizen.*

Long story short: the women loved Canadians; hated the Canadian car culture. "We were tourists in your country for five weeks," Chabowski wrote. "Our overwhelming memory of Canada is cars, traffic, parking and the related obesity and unfulfilled communities. We were treated like second-class citizens compared to cars. The air was dirty and the constant noise from horns and engines was unpleasant."

Of all the nerve. I find Ms. Chabowski's comments rude, impertinent, unsettling and unseemly.

Too bad she's dead right.

A goldfish never figures out that it lives in a glass bowl. North Americans don't seem to notice that we live in a world customized for stinking, cacophonous, resource-guzzling, lethal motorized conveyances. Some day ages hence historians will look back and shake their heads at the way we allowed mere vehicles to dictate how we lived. They'll find it hard to accept that we fouled our own air, gutted our cities for freeways, paved farmland for suburbs and cloverleafs and built multi-storey parking garages to house two-tonne machines, many of which were only used a couple of hours a day.

Perhaps it takes a Holly Chabowski to open our eyes. She grew up in cities that were built before the car took over. Europeans must have an instinctive appreciation for non-car culture, right?

Well . . . I'm not sure. There is, after all, Västerås. It's a typical small town not known for much other than that one insane weekend each summer when masses of chrome and steel land yachts, many of them more than half a century old, show up for a phenomenon called Power Big Meet. Which just happens to be the biggest—and possibly grossest—automobile show in the world.

Eighteen thousand cars showed up for Power Big Meet in July 2014. Not sleek Aston Martins, dinky Smart cars or even stodgy Volvos. They were great hulking Pontiacs, Fords, Oldsmobiles and Chevrolets. Detroit behemoths of 1960s' and 1970s' vintage.

In North America such cars are considered beaters, junkers and gas-guzzling dinosaurs.

In Västerås they call them pure gold. They say that for that one weekend there's more classic Detroit iron in the tiny town of Västerås than in all of the United States. They celebrate their clunkers with drag races, car parades, very loud country music . . . and they drink an awful lot of beer.

Sounds a lot like a Down South tailgate party but Power Big Meet happens a little north and east of Dixie. Västerås is a small town an hour's drive north of Stockholm. That's Stockholm . . . Sweden.

You know Sweden . . . Denmark's next-door neighbour?

Don't look now, Holly Chabowski, but your goldfish bowl is showing.

The USA, She Is A-Changin'

*M*ake no mistake about it. Noah Kilpatrick is a victim of discrimination. The 15-year-old student at the Faith Fellowship Christian School in Waterdown, New York, has been relentlessly bullied and denigrated, not just by his fellow students but by members of the school faculty. "They told me that (my people) were all stupid," Kilpatrick recalls. He says they insulted his home and made fun of his country.

It's a familiar story, alas. First Nations people know the experience only too well, as do Latinos and African Americans. I grew up in a time when Italians were routinely referred to as wops, Frenchmen were frogs, Chinese were chinks and the English were limeys (or, to my Oz friends, pommy bastards).

But that's not Noah Kilpatrick's problem. He's not First Nations or of European extraction. Nor does he have roots in Africa or South America.

Noah Kilpatrick's lineage problem is—he's Canadian.

For some reason, two of the teachers (one of them is also the principal) started ragging on Noah because he was born in Canada.

"They'd say things like, 'Canada's full of communists. They

club baby seals.' That my opinion doesn't really matter because I'm a Canadian."

Not to be paranoid or anything but you have to wonder if somebody isn't slipping moron pills into the Faith Fellowship School water supply. Quite apart from the fact that this is a Christian school in the land of the free persecuting a 15-year-old kid, it's just plain, well, out of date. The trash-talking students and faculty are seriously behind the American learning curve.

They may snicker at Canada but the rest of the USA is running as fast as it can to catch up to us.

Consider: in the past few months American legislators have been locked in courtroom battles to legalize gay marriage, marijuana use and amnesty for immigrants.

Canadians? Been there. Done that.

Gun control? Wild West insanity in the US while in Canada, no problem, eh? We don't go postal about our right to bear arms. Are we different than Americans? You bet your health care card and Cowichan sweater we are. Two researchers, Canadian Michael Adams and American Celinda Lake, have been studying attitudes in the two countries for the past 20 years. They have concluded that we are indeed drawing closer to one another.

Ironically, the change is almost exclusively on the US side.

Americans (notwithstanding Neolithic loons like George W., Rush Limbaugh and the Tea Party) are systematically embracing more liberal social values every year.

Americans have seen the light. They're becoming more like us.

But not fast enough for the Kilpatricks. Even though they've lived in Waterdown for a decade his mother has pulled Noah out of school. "No fifteen-year-old should have to question his self-worth at the hands of a teacher," she says. He'll finish his Grade 9 at home. After that they'll probably move back to Ottawa.

Good move, folks. Seems like your slice of America is just a little too backward to "get" Canada.

Grab the Money and Run

*The salary of the chief executive of a large
corporation is not a market award for achievement. It
is frequently in the nature of a warm personal gesture
by the individual to himself.*

JOHN KENNETH GALBRAITH

Old J.K.G. was America's most famous Canadian—their greatest economist and a leading light in the Kennedy administration as well as a career diplomat used to rubbing elbows with the world's Extremely Well-off elite. For those of us without a mug in which to micturate, it's comforting to think that the wealthy few are a pack of incestuous scuzzbuckets who will ultimately roast in hell. Heaven knows some of them have earned it.

Take Antony Jenkins. As Chief Executive Officer of Barclays Bank in England it was Mr. Jenkins' painful duty recently to announce the layoffs of more than 12,000 employees.

Mr. Jenkins barely had time to whip off the black armband and don a party hat before announcing a top-up to the bonus pool for Barclays executives of $345 million.

That's just the one-year increase. The total Barclays bonus pool (make that small inland sea) is 2.38 billion British pounds—close to $4 billion US. That's about three times the amount Barclays paid out in dividends last year.

The upper crust of our own Royal Bank is much more conservative. Its CEO, Gord Nixon, permitted himself only a hummingbird sip of the company coffers last year. A modest increase of a mere 1 percent. Very humble. Very Canadian.

Mind you it did bring his paycheque up to $12.7 million.

Almost 13 million dollars. For one year's work.

Pardon me for asking, but who in hell needs $12.7 million dollars a year? That's $250,000 a week.

Put another way, every time Gord goes for a leak in the RBC corporate washroom he makes 6,250 bucks.

Even more if he stops to comb his hair.

Such a salary is obscene, amoral and profoundly anti-social. It doesn't reflect the behaviour of a pillar of society; it's the MO of a Somali sea pirate.

Not all tycoons are unrepentant greed heads. I know of a guy so rich he could buy and sell Gord Nixon before breakfast. He could buy himself a small country if he cared to but he doesn't. Instead he and his wife have put together a worldwide charitable foundation dedicated to making things better for the bottom of the bottom of the world's 99 percent.

What's more, he's optimistic about the future. He says the world economy is getting better. "I am so optimistic," he says, "that I am willing to make a prediction: by 2035, there will be almost no poor countries left in the world."

This guy knows a thing or two about making money. His name is Bill Gates.

J.K. Galbraith once observed: "The greater the wealth, the thicker the dirt."

Not always, J.K. Not always.

The Canada That Almost Was

I don't know what they teach high school kids about Canadian history these days. I can only hope it's better than what I learned. Or rather, didn't learn.

My teachers glossed over the first few thousand years, for starters. First Nations people had been here since the retreat of the glaciers but I was taught that history began with the arrival of the Europeans. "Indians" appeared in the pages of my history texts as faithful companions, handy guides and trading partner patsies, eager to exchange valuable furs for trinkets and baubles.

There were some gaps and omissions in the White Man side of the ledger too. Cabot and Champlain got plenty of ink, as did Alexander Mackenzie and Simon Fraser.

But how did my teachers miss the story of La Galissonière? Roland-Michel Barrin de La Galissonière, to give him his full and magnificent moniker. A handle like that alone should get you a place in the history books, but I never heard of the man until last month.

Monsieur La G. and North America didn't intersect until 1747 when he was appointed governor of New France. He was a commander in the French navy at the time and can't have been delighted to be sent to the snow-swept shores of the St. Lawrence.

Or perhaps he was. La Galissonière appears to have been the kind of man who, if handed a lemon, made lemon daiquiris. Despite limited resources (the French really didn't give much a damn about their "few acres of snow" in the far-off colony) La Galissonière dispatched teams to chart the coasts of Newfoundland, Acadia and Ile Royale. He also sent officers into the interior with instructions to "observe, collect, chart, record and otherwise thoroughly document" the natural history of the interior. They were specifically enjoined to peacefully engage with the natives in order to woo them to the French side of the Anglo-Franco seesaw.

La Galissonière was, of all governmental rarities, a bureaucrat with an insatiable scientific curiosity. He sought to learn and document everything he could about this new, largely unknown land.

So, naturally, his superiors fired him.

Recalled him, actually. La Galissonière spent only two short years—1747 to 1749—in New France. He would go on to other postings where he would exercise his itch for knowledge: he appointed missions to chart the coasts of Spain, Portugal and Madeira, even to catalogue the stars in the southern hemisphere. But the fledgling colony that would eventually become the nucleus of Canada was returned to the care of number crunchers and political time-servers more interested in furthering their careers than nurturing a nation.

Two and a half centuries later we live with a "governor" Harper, who purges scientific libraries and gags government scientists, preventing them from speaking publicly about what our taxes pay for them to do.

I don't know how the history books will portray our times, but I'm reasonably certain that Roland-Michel Barrin de La Galissonière is spinning in his grave.

Call Me Lefty? All Right By Me

So there I was, about to sit down and watch a movie called *The United States of Amnesia*, a documentary about Gore Vidal, the famously gay, famously prickly American novelist/screenwriter/commentator and scourge of all things Tea Baggish and crypto-Nazoid concerning the USA.

As the film is set to roll a guy turns to me and says, "You? What are you doing here? I thought you were a right winger!"

Right winger? Moi? Don't think so, comrade.

I'm definitely to the windward side of Marx, Lenin, Mao, Pol Pot and Fidel but that doesn't mean I'd care to break bread with Caligula, Attila, Sarah Palin or the brothers Koch.

In any case, Gore Vidal was a cross-cultural giant who transcended such petty classifications. This is the wit who once stood up before television cameras to tell the world some devastating news: the previous night Ronald Reagan's Presidential Library had burned to the ground.

"Such a tragedy," Vidal deadpanned solemnly. "Both books were destroyed and President Reagan hadn't even finished colouring one of them."

Left wing, right wing—who cares when you can deliver a line like that?

It's a weird and outdated designation anyway, the left/right thing. We stole the template from the French Legislative Assembly where, about 200 years ago, monarchists were accustomed to sit on the right side of the assembly hall, while the anti-monarchists occupied the left side. From that we formed the concept that anything conservative (Republican, Whig, Tory, traditionalist, Loyalist, High Anglican, tight-assed) perched on the right wing of the political jumbo jet, while anything liberal (Grit, progressive, agnostic, reformist, socialist, communist, squishy) rode the left wing.

It turns out there may be physiological justification for the left/right political divide. Researchers at University College in London got 90 volunteers to rate themselves on a spectrum ranging from Very Conservative to Very Liberal. Then they all received MRI scans.

Not to get too scientific but the correlation was stunning. Conservatives, it seems, have larger right amygdala—an area of the brain associated with fear and anxiety. Liberals have larger anterior cingulated cortexes—part of the brain that handles nuances and complexities. Put crudely, conservatives are more prone to make decisions based on nervous apprehension; liberals are inclined to take a, well, more liberal approach.

Hey—no judgement here, pal; I'm just putting it out there.

If the fact that I'd rather have a coffee with Mike Royko than Stephen Harper makes me liberal, then call me Lefty.

Mike Royko? He's the guy who said, "It's easier to be a conservative than a liberal because it's easier to give the finger than a helping hand."

This Mayor May Not Be True

Wally Assef did NOT pat the Queen's bum.

Not that it would have been much of a stretch. Wally was mayor of Thunder Bay at the time of the alleged incident and even as Canadian mayors go, Wally was a pratfall waiting to happen.

It's not exactly a Machiavellian job, being mayor. Snip a few ribbons, shake some hands, smile a lot, keep your hands clean and your pants up and you'll muddle through.

Not. Look at some of the characters Canadians have voted into office: Winnipeg mayor Sam Katz, accused of trying to write off a $3,000 bill for a staff Christmas party at a restaurant owned by—oops!—mayor Sam Katz.

Hazel McCallion, perennial mayor of Mississauga, accused of influencing a real estate decision that tipped $11 million to a company owned by—oops!—Hazel McCallion's son.

The list goes on. London mayor Joe Fontana, charged with fraud. Laval mayor Gilles Vaillancourt, accused of accepting payoffs. Montreal mayor Gerald Tremblay, tainted with corruption charges. Halifax mayor Peter Kelly, accused of questionable ethics involving the estate of an elderly client.

Ottawa mayor Larry O'Brien candidly admitted that his first two years in office were "a complete disaster."

And then there's Toronto, with its history of mayoral oddities. Anyone out there old enough to remember Lampy? Allan Lamport was mayor of Toronto for just two years (1952–54) but he ruled in style, moving into a suite at the Royal York and racking up nearly $400,000 for room service (champagne, cigars, gourmet dinners and booze for Lampy and his buddies).

All on the taxpayer's tab.

Not so long ago Mel ("Noooobody!") Lastman, wearing the chain of office and an unlikely rug, immortalized Toronto for the rest of Canada by pleading for the Canadian Armed Forces to help Torontonians through a snowstorm.

As for Toronto's last mayor . . . what's left to say? Mayor Ford hammered out his own headlines almost daily.

Okay, I'll say this: If Rob Ford were ever to run for the mayor's office again there's a block of voters he could count on: columnists. Rob Ford is copy gold. Most newspaper scribblers would auction their mothers to have Ford on their speed dial.

I know. I was a newspaper columnist in Thunder Bay for most of the seventies and eighties when Wally Assef was mayor. "Jolly Wally" was a bald, chubby, five-foot-nothing Lebanese-Canadian firecracker who was not always jolly. He had a fuse that was even shorter than he was, he shot from the lip and never met a speech he couldn't mangle.

When the Queen visited Thunder Bay in 1974 Wally officially thanked Prince Philip for bringing "his good wife" to the Lakehead.

But he did not, as legend has it, pat the Queen's bum. That is a base canard invented by a drunken journalist (not this one) over schooners of Kakabeka Cream Lager at the Thunder Bay Press Club.

I know. I was there. Not at the press club—at the royal reception. Somebody must have tipped Prince Philip off about the mayor's meandering mitts because Phil watched Wally like a hawk. Wally's hands never got near the royal end zone.

Kind of appropriate, that: a British hawk watching for a Canada goose.

You Know What Dogs Do to Poles

It's tough to make predictions. Especially about the future.

YOGI BERRA

*W*ith all due respect to the famously tongue-tied American baseball player, he was wrong on this call. Predicting the future is dead easy; predicting it accurately is somewhat trickier. These days few know this better than Canada's professional forecasters—Ipsos Reid, Angus Reid and Forum Research, among others. Perhaps you can see them over there, cringing in the dugout, their tails between their legs. These poor wretches haven't had innings this bad since then Prime Minister John Diefenbaker locked his eyes on a pollster and thundered, "Polls? Polls? You know what dogs do to poles!"

In 2012 the pollsters struck out forecasting the provincial elections in Alberta and Quebec. In 2013 they whiffed spectacularly on the British Columbia election. A few months before British Columbians went to the ballot box the oracles were supremely confident, not a doubt in their neatly tabulated minds. The advance polls had been conducted, the results had been collated and it was all over but the congratulatory popping of champagne corks. The Liberals under Christy Clark were headed for the bone yard, they said. The NDP was a shoo-in. Sixty-three percent of polled British Columbians disapproved of the job Clark was doing. Sixty-one percent said they wanted a change in government. The NDP had a 17-point lead going in. How could they lose?

But lose they did. Clark's Liberals crushed them. Somebody forgot to tell the BC voters to follow the script.

I am not crowing about this because I, too, believed Christy Clark and the Liberals were toast. I followed the polls and listened to the pundits and lustily sang from the same songbook. I should have remembered the words of John Kenneth Galbraith. "There are two classes of people who tell us what's going to happen in the future," said Galbraith. "Those who don't know and those who don't know they don't know."

Embarrassingly, I find myself in both categories.

But not as embarrassed, I think, as the editor of the *Chicago Daily Tribune* who wrote the headline that ran on the November 3, 1948 edition of that paper.

DEWEY DEFEATS TRUMAN, it read.

You have probably seen a photograph of this famous newspaper front page. It's in all the history books and it's usually being held aloft.

By a grinning, president-elect Harry S. Truman.

"Put not your faith in rulers," the Bible says. Same goes for soothsayers, crystal ball gazers, psychics, fortune tellers, prestidigitators, voodooists, witch doctors—and political pollsters. "Poll-taking," said E.B. White, "is not a science at all, but necromancy. People are unpredictable by nature, and although you can take a nation's pulse, you can't be sure a nation hasn't just run up a flight of stairs."

And for errant pollsters, judgement is merciless. The story goes that shortly after the Truman–Dewey upset, the famous US opinion sampler George Gallup was stopped by a policeman for driving down a one-way street in the wrong direction. When he read the name on Gallup's driving licence, the cop whooped and hollered, "Wrong again!"

Where Poppies Blow

*L*et's hear it for Joel Poinsett and Caspar Wistar. And a hand for J.G. Zinn, Anders Dahl and Leonhart Fuchs as well.

What's special about those dudes? They all have flowers named after them, to wit: poinsettia, wisteria, zinnia, dahlia and fuchsia. What could be more sublime than knowing that a beautiful bloom will bear your name forever?

Johann Friedrich von Eschscholtz has that honour. The genus *Eschscholzia* of the family Papaveraceae is named after the nineteenth-century Russian scientist. We know it better as the California poppy.

Which brings us, in a rambling, creeping vine sort of way, to the subject of the day: the poppy. We mostly know the red kind, *Papaver rhoeas*, which we wear on our lapels each November, but the poppy can come in any colour and a bewildering variety of guises. It can grow up to four feet tall; the blossoms can be the size of a dinner plate.

Aside from Herr Eschscholtz's namesake there is the Prickly, the Welsh, the Pygmy, the Wind, the Tulip, the Tree and the Desert Bearpaw variety.

Poppies are a weed that grow anywhere from the plains of India to the battlefields of Flanders to the front lawn of the

RCMP detachment on Salt Spring Island (really). And the flowers go back a ways. Early Greeks and Romans used them as offerings to their dead. Ancient Egyptian medicos ground up the seeds and fed them to patients for pain relief. And somewhere along the line somebody discovered that if you cultivated the right species of poppy and harvested it at the right time, you got an industrial-strength pain reliever: opium. Later they discovered it was also lethally addictive.

So they dumped it on the Chinese.

Rather, the British East India Trading Company did. Back in the early 1800s British merchants found themselves with a huge cash crop of opium distilled from the poppy fields of India. They shipped it off to China (ignoring the protests of the Chinese emperor who had banned the drug).

The British got filthy rich; China got generations of junkies and eventually endured the Opium Wars in which tens of thousands (almost all Chinese) were killed.

Free trade, nineteenth-century style.

Fast forward to Afghanistan at the end of the twentieth century. Under the Taliban, Afghan poppy farmers (who supplied 75 percent of the world's opium) were put out of business on pain of death.

That was then. A little over a decade later Afghan poppies are once again blowing in the wind. And 2013 marked the third record year for production of (ahem) non-pharmaceutical grade opiates, 92 percent of which come from Afghanistan.

The poppy. A beautiful flower that inspired "In Flanders Fields," the most famous poem ever written by a Canadian. A flower of peace and remembrance.

But a flower with a history as blood-soaked red as the petals of a *Papaver rhoeas*.

A House of Sober Second Thought. On Second Thought . . .

*H*ollywood blessed us with the Keystone Kops. Britain tossed in *The Goon Show* and *Monty Python's Flying Circus*. France gave us Monsieur Hulot. Canada's contribution to slapstick comedy? That's easy—it's that national punching bag for comedians, cartoonists and water cooler wisenheimers from Prince Rupert to Joe Batt's Arm. Perhaps Canada's longest-running (if least funny) comedy ensemble: the Canadian Senate.

There's an old joke about the difference between an American senator and a Canadian one: in America you have to win an election to become a senator; in Canada you have to lose one. But that's not true. You don't even have to be a failed politician to become a Canadian senator; you merely have to make sure your IOU is firmly lodged in the prime minister's pocket. Party hacks get Senate seats. So do backroom bagmen, union functionaries, First Nations figureheads and long-in-the-tooth loyalists notable only for their reflexive genuflections toward 24 Sussex.

Margaret Atwood called our senate a featherbed for fallen Liberals but the Tories are no slouches when it comes to rewarding the faithful. Mr. Mulroney was a deft hand at dealing out Get-into-the-Senate-Free cards. Stephen Harper's a relative newcomer but already he's appointed more than a third of the members.

Yes, many of those appointed have served nobly and well, but the pork—oops—apple barrel only needs a worm or two to spoil the works, and since its inception the Canadian Senate has been riddled with shysters, charlatans, buffoons and blockheads.

But at least we've never had to deal with a Senator Incitatus.

Now THERE was a political appointee that put the pork in pork barrelling. No Duffy-esque Cavendish cottage for Senator Incitatus; no $350,000 per year travel budget à la Ms. Wallin. You kidding? Chump change for Senator Incitatus.

This is a stud who had his entire office gilded in marble. Everything he ate was served to him on hand-carved ivory. For public appearances he wore garlands of priceless gems. He had a permanent staff of 18 who worked like slaves for him. And gold? He ate the stuff.

Really. The emperor Caligula decreed that Senator Incitatus have gold leaf mixed in with his, er, oats.

Incitatus was a chariot-racing stallion. His stable was made of marble, his manger was carved out of ivory and he really was a Roman senator. His owner, Caligula, (who did he think he was—Stephen Harper?) installed him in the Roman senate back in 39 AD.

We learned in school that Senator Incitatus was proof of Caligula's lunacy. And the man was a lunatic—a monster who murdered at whim, committed incest with all three sisters and had himself declared "a Living God."

Crazy for sure, but crazy enough to make his horse a senator?

Crazy like a fox, say some historians. They point out that the Roman senate (like others we've heard of) was a mere rubber stamp endorsing those in power. They suggest that Caligula's equine senator was really a subtle insult to the most famously gelded political body in Rome.

Canadians are too shy for such bold gestures. We'd never think of installing an actual horse in our senate.

Just the hindquarters.

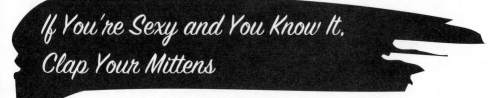

If You're Sexy and You Know It, Clap Your Mittens

*I*t happened again. Craig Ferguson, the glottally immoderate Glaswegian-American ex-host of *The Late Late Show*, winked at the TV cameras and intoned: "Canada is not the parrrrty. It's the aparrrrtment above the parrrrrty."

Ah, yes. The Canada-as-stodgy-klutz-in-earmuffs-and-mukluks trope. Never get tired of that joke.

How did this happen? How did the perception crystallize that America is hip and cool while Canada is like your Baptist uncle at the wedding reception trying to limbo in a Tilley fedora with Sansabelt trousers hiked up to his nipples?

America hip? The USA cool? I've got two words for you, neighbour.

Spitzer and Weiner.

Those are America's latest candidates for the Sex Scandal Hall of Infamy. Elliot Spitzer, ex-New York governor, caught by the FBI with his pants down in the company of a series of call girls (he even left a thousand-dollar deposit with an escort company for "future business") and Anthony Weiner, ex-US congressman, whose idea of being a smooth operator is sexting close-ups of his junk trunk to, well, a blackjack dealer, a porn actress and a cheer-leading coach, among others.

This is suave and urbane? Listen, cousin. We may not be as let-it-all-hang-out raunchy as you folks but at least we Canucks know how to do a sex scandal properly.

Take Gerda Munsinger.

Oh, you can't. The curvaceous blonde siren was deported back to East Germany in 1961 following RCMP revelations that she'd cavorted with half of John Diefenbaker's cabinet, including Canada's national minister of defence, Pierre Sevigny. Oh, and it looks as if she wasn't just a good-time girl, she was probably a Soviet spy, to boot.

Or how about those stuffy Brits? Tory war minister Sir John Profumo engaged in pillow talk with Christine Keeler while a cohort rifled his briefcase in search of nuclear warhead secrets. If memory serves, Christine was also doing mattress time with a Soviet naval attaché/spy named Ivanov.

Those aren't grubby little backroom sex scandals; those are plots for two unmade James Bond movies.

But when it comes to grubby little backroom sex scandals the entire world must take a backseat to the US. Let me be sure I have the details of your most famous high-profile sexcapade correct, America.

No, no—I'm not talking about serial swordsman JFK, who seldom saw a skirt he didn't lift and even sank to "dates" set up by Chicago mobster Sam "Momo" Giancana—I meant the other presidential sexcapade. President Clinton, wasn't it? With a 20-something intern? In a closet off the Oval Office? While slices of pizza cooled and curled in a takeout box nearby?

Classy.

Comedian Jon Stewart once cracked, "I've been to Canada, and I've always gotten the impression that I could take the country over in about two days."

Al Capone, feigning ignorance of cross-border booze smuggling, once assured investigators, "I don't even know what street Canada is on."

Keep talking, wise guys. Keep it up with the bada-bing

bada-boom rim shots, the forked-tongue asides, the knowing sneers. Sensitivity has never been your long suit but you've always been a dab hand at frat boy digs. Every dog has his day and sooner or later your Rottweiler snarl will land your Chihuahua ass in a sling.

You better hope it happens on our side of the border. That way our medicare might cover your hospital bill.

Part 8

WRITE THIS WAY, FOLKS

Of Elmore and Bill

One of the head scratchers about English literature is the number of famous books around that nobody reads. Did you read last year's winner of the Man Booker Prize? Neither did I. Do you even remember who it was? Same here. A lot of people, myself included, bought a copy of Salman Rushdie's *The Satanic Verses*. Did you ever try to read it? My begrudging compliments to the psychopathic mullahs who laid a death threat on Rushdie for writing it. Whatever their sins they managed to read enough of the book to be outraged.

James Joyce is lauded as a prose master but if you threw a party for everyone who honestly made it past page 14 of *Finnegans Wake*, two large pizzas would probably cover your food requirements.

Most writers appeal to a narrow slice of the audience. Ezra Pound's *Cantos* are great fun for literati who savour a Greek pun leavened by a medieval Italian aphorism, while Dan Brown (*The Da Vinci Code*) satisfies readers who move their lips when they read.

Very few writers are good enough to please everyone—book snobs and bellhops, genius and jerk. Dickens comes close but he wore too much purple and never met an adjective he didn't like.

In the end I can think of only two. One of them died nearly 400 years ago; the other died more recently.

William Shakespeare hardly needs an introduction. Sixteen tragedies, ten histories, twelve comedies plus a raft of poems, all culled from his teeming brain with a quill pen on parchment. Though the English language has since morphed and evolved, his works are still performed in his original words every year all around the world, from the London stage to Australian outback music halls; on a beach in Vancouver and under the white lights of Broadway.

The other master writer? Elmore Leonard, a Detroit boy, dead of a stroke in 2013 at 87. He wrote more than 40 novels, most of them about crooks, but it would be a mistake to dismiss him as a "crime writer." He was, as the *New Yorker* said, "one of the best writers who happened to write about crime."

It took the world a while to catch on. He didn't make the best-seller list until he was 60 and his first crime novel, *The Big Bounce*, was rejected 84 times. But he was world famous long before he died—and largely unmoved by it. Critics raved about his "ear for dialogue." Leonard shrugged. "People always say, 'Where do you get your characters' words?' And I say, 'Can't you remember people talking or think up people talking in your head?' That's all it is. I don't know why that seems such a wonderment to people."

But wonderment it was in Elmore's hands. His fans are legion. One of them wrote of the novel *Glitz*: "This is the kind of book that if you get up to see if there are any chocolate chip cookies left, you take it with you so you won't miss anything."

Chap named Steven King said that.

As for writerly advice, Leonard kept that sweet and simple too. "Don't go into great detail describing places and things," he advised.

And my favourite: "Try to leave out the parts that readers tend to skip."

Writers, there you have it. Now go and write a classic.

Dropping the A-Word

*A*wesome. From Shakespeare's time the word has meant exactly what it said: something that inspires awe.

A sky full of towering thunderheads stitched with jagged bolts of lightning—that would be awesome. A forest fire at its furious worst—definitely awesome. So too a military barrage, a waterfall, a field of golden wheat winnowed by the wind.

And awesome needn't be enormous. The transformation of a caterpillar into a monarch butterfly is decidedly awesome, as is the exoskeleton of a cricket or the machinations of a honeybee. The guts of a humble wristwatch are awesome to behold and "awesome" fits a Bach prelude like an ivory-hilted stiletto in a doeskin sheath.

A grand word, awesome, and it has served us well. But somewhere along the way the word mutated, morphed and bloated into semantic meaninglessness.

This morning in a coffee shop I said, "I'll have a medium coffee, black, please." "Awesome," the barista said.

No. No, that's not awesome. As cups of coffee go it turned out to be not half bad, but "okay" is several light years from "awesome."

Over the past little while I've been informed by, or overheard people affirming that: they've purchased an awesome T-shirt; watched an awesome commercial; eaten an awesome hamburger; and met an awesome real estate agent. I'd like to believe that all these experiences were as jaw-droppingly life altering as the adjective "awesome'" implies. But somehow I doubt it.

Exuberance is an admirable quality but it's a seasoning, not a staple food. Too much relish can ruin a perfectly adequate hot dog.

The hyper-inflating trajectory of the word awesome reminds me of the early twentieth century Deutschmark. One day the German currency was hardy and stable, worth the equivalent of a modern Canadian loony, give or take. The next day a wheelbarrow full of thousand-Deutschmark banknotes wouldn't buy you a bratwurst.

"Awesome" is undergoing the linguistic equivalent right now. There is a book in your local bookstore called *The Book of Awesome.* You'll find it sitting cheek by jowl with another book entitled *The Book of Even More Awesom*e.

Call me prophetic, but I foresee future bestsellers with names like *The Even Awesomer Book of Awesome* and *Son of Book of Awesome Take Two: The Sequel.*

It's not just books. There is an Awesome Foundation in San Francisco. In Massachusetts there is an Institute of Higher Awesome Studies. How long before some entrepreneur brings out the Awesome potato peeler, Awesome detergent or Awesome chewing gum?

You know what I think? I think it would be refreshing to sequester the word "awesome" for a spell. Give it a time out, a sabbatical, a little shore leave. We've got lots of bench strength to take up the slack—we could always buy a "splendid" T-shirt, watch a "hilarious" commercial, eat a "delicious" hamburger and meet a "mesmerizing" real estate agent. The A-word could be resting in rehab, regaining its former lustre and glory.

Now that would be truly awesome.

Standing On Our Own Feet

You put your right foot in, you put your right foot out.
You put your right foot in, and you shake it all about.

Canada has officially been a metric nation for more than 40 years.

I still don't get it.

I continue to think in inches, feet and yards; I feel in Fahrenheit. A beautiful day is 75 and sunny; a miserable one is 10 below with driving snow.

I'm partially converted. I recognize a metre as a yard-and-a-bit; a kilometre is half a mile, give or take.

I wouldn't know a hectare from the Higgs boson particle.

But it's not just reactionary codgerism at work here. I'm a writer. Words excite me and the metric system is as mind grindingly boring as a Stephen Harper stump speech.

Our old tried-and-true system had cables, rods, fathoms, gills, pecks and acres. In metric, "gram" is a racy outlier; everything else is milli, centi or kilo something.

Accurate, yes. But hardly the stuff that poems are made of:

> *Two-point-four kilometres, two-point-four kilometres, two-point-four kilometres onward,*

Into the valley of Death rode the six hundred.

Or perhaps what Shakespeare really meant when he wrote,

"Full fathom five, your father lies; his bones of coral made,"
was: *"Full nine-point-one-four metres your father lies . . ."*

Why, my right foot contains more lyricism than the entire metric system. I can have itchy feet, feet of clay, one foot in the grave or two left feet. I can get off on the right foot or be caught with my foot in my mouth. I can trip over my own feet or shoot myself in the foot. I might choose to put my foot down to take charge, put my feet up to relax, put my foot in the door or wait on someone hand and foot.

Or I can be a heel. Or cool my heels as I wait for the bus, dig in my heels to be obstinate, bring somebody to heel who's giving me grief or even expose my nautical Achilles heel by allowing my sailboat to heel over in a squall.

One of my favourite activities: to go outside on a clear night and watch the stars dance heel and toe.

Which brings us to the other pedal extremities—the toes. To stay on one's toes means to look sharp; to tread on someone's toes means to interfere with someone. On the other hand if I toe the line I'm minding my manners.

Not to mention putting my best foot forward.

Yessir, those boney flippers attached to your ankles are a treasure trove of linguistic possibilities. You think the metric system has anything comparable to offer?

My foot it does.

So You Want to Be a Writer

There are three rules for writing a novel.
Unfortunately, no one knows what they are.
SOMERSET MAUGHAM

The business of writing fiction for a living is altogether strange. The fiction writer is not like the farmer with his seeds, the soldier with his rifle, the teacher with her curriculum or the violinist with her Stradivarius. The writer has only what's between the ears—and whatever can be coaxed to bubble up and be set down on the page.

And even if the fiction writer strikes literary gold there's still the chancy, grubby business of getting it published. I know of one writer who toiled for years over what he thought was his master-piece, only to be metaphorically kicked in the teeth over and over again.

He couldn't even find a North American publisher at first, so in desperation he sent his manuscript to an agent in Britain. He got the book published all right. Quite a nice job actually, in three handsome volumes.

Unfortunately, the publisher managed to somehow lose the ending of the book—the epilogue—which rather ruined the effect.

Not surprisingly, the British critics were less than kind.

"An ill-compounded mixture of romance and matter-of-fact," wrote one. "The idea of a connected and collected story has obviously visited and abandoned its writer again and again in the course of composition. The style of his tale is in places disfigured by mad (rather than bad) English; and its catastrophe is hastily, weakly, and obscurely managed."

Harsh words, but delicious to the ears of North American literary reviewers who reprinted the British reviews without bothering to, you know, actually read the book they were trashing. The bad press was disastrous; the author was deeply in debt and praying that the book would earn enough money to placate the bill collectors.

But to be absolutely fair, the book he'd written was a bit . . . odd. It was written in highly stylized, at times baffling language with dollops of symbolism and lashings of metaphor. It dealt with, among many other themes, madness, murder and mass slaughter, of both men and animals. At times the author printed stage directions as if a play was being performed. His main character was an animal, for heaven's sake—an albino, in fact, which thought and acted like a sadistic human stalker.

Stephen King might be able to pull off a plot like that, but this author wasn't Stephen King and the times—the mid-nineteenth century—certainly weren't propitious for such an outlandish and unlikely tale.

Nevertheless, the author—unfamiliar with the rules of novel writing—persisted and finally found an American publisher who was willing to take a flyer. In 1851 Harper and Brothers of New York published a North American edition.

The book was a dud—mostly because of those critical British reviews. The author, they say, never really recovered from his failure and died an unhappy, debt-ridden failure.

Pity he didn't live a little longer. The author's name was Herman Melville and his book, *Moby Dick*, is now considered a classic.

Strange business, writing fiction.

A Rabbi, a Priest and a Duck Go into a Bar

*B*less me, Groucho, for I have sinned. I told a Polish joke in a speech. It was harmless enough, I thought. Few people laughed but I often get that reaction when I tell a joke. I thought no more about it—until someone took me aside and murmured in my ear, "Did you see the look on K's face when you told that joke? She was stricken! She's Polish you know."

Omigawd! Now it was me who was stricken. I had no intention of hurting anybody's feelings. It never crossed my mind that the joke could be construed as offensive. I've been telling jokes about cheap Scots, drunken Irishmen, pompous Germans and stuffy Brits for decades. Not once has anyone objected. Occasionally they even laughed.

I writhed in guilt. I groaned in agony. I considered a new wardrobe of sackcloth, ashes and a penitential riding crop for self-flagellation. I composed a belly-crawling *mea culpa* email explaining my remorse, begging forgiveness, professing nothing but the highest respect—and sent it off to K.

Almost immediately an email popped up in my Inbox with her name on it. With trembling fingers I tapped the "open" button.

"Good grief!" she wrote. "What a puzzlement!" Not only had she not taken offence, she didn't even remember the joke.

Boiled down, K's advice about the incident was: "Take a chill pill, pal."

We live in an era of political correctness and it's made us all a little gun shy. (Trusting I didn't offend anyone in the National Rifle Association with that metaphor.)

In Portland, Oregon, a school principal has banned references to peanut butter and jam sandwiches, deeming the term "culturally insensitive to children of other cultures."

In Australia, new guidelines suggest that calling someone "normal" is offensive to people with, you know, um, what used to be called handicaps. From now on, the correct term for a "normal" Ozzie is "a non-disabled person."

And speaking of handicaps—please don't. The term has been declared offensive. Not to "differently-abled" persons—to street people, who are often observed "cap in hand."

Please bear in mind I am not making any of this up.

The next day I found another email in my Inbox. "World's Best Ethnic Joke," it was called. It went like this:

"An Englishman, a Scotsman, an Irishman, a Welshman, a Newfie, an Inuit, a lesbian, a rabbi, a Catholic priest, a Muslim imam, a blonde, a Ukrainian, a midget, a Gabriola Islander, a Laotian, a Cambodian, a North Vietnamese and a South Vietnamese walk into a five-star Parisian restaurant.

"The snooty maître d' examines the group disdainfully then holds up a hand and says, 'I am varee sorry, but even zo you 'ave a Cambodian, a Laotian and two Vietnamese in your group . . .

"I cannot let you in wizzout a Thai.'"

The email was from K.

In Praise of "The Sticks"

I'd rather wake up in the middle of nowhere than in any city on earth.

STEVE MCQUEEN

All my life I've stood on the sidelines of a titanic battle between the City and the Country. Now it's official: the City has won.

Not for me personally. I'm still a country bumpkin who lives many green and verdant miles from the nearest stoplight, billboard or high-rise, but worldwide, I'm grasping the short end of the stick. Humans—nearly all 7.3 billion of us—are flocking to cities like fruit flies to an overripe kumquat. In 1950 there were only 2 cities in the world with populations over 10 million. By 2007 there were 19. The UN estimates that within a dozen years, 27 cities will top the 10 million mark. As I write, there are 90 cities in China alone that host more than a million citizens each.

The tipping point was 2008. Since that year the world has officially had more people living in cities than in rural areas. According to Laurence Smith, author of a book called *The World in 2050*, cities in the developing world have been collectively bloating by about three million people per week. That, says Smith, is the equivalent of adding one more Seattle to the planet every day. Worldwide, farmers and farm workers are becoming obsolete. Think of it: for the first time in history most humans have no physical ability to grow their own food or supply their own water.

I can't be the only one who finds that ominous.

Mind you, it's not as if we're running out of real estate for all these cities. Experts say all of humanity could fit into a space the size of Alberta—each with a personal townhouse, in fact. But we lose an awful lot with mass urbanization.

Just about everything I hold dear, actually. My city friends sometimes ask me if I don't get lonely living in the country. I tell them that I only feel lonely on subway trains and in airports. They ask, "But don't you find it boring? Unstimulating?"

I refer them to a lady we all know who spent four decades living in the boonies of rural Canada. She went about her business with her eyes open and her ears cocked.

From what she saw and heard she wrote 14 books crammed with short stories about the rural world around her.

"I don't think I'd have been nearly so brave a writer if I'd lived in town and if I had gone to school with other people who were interested in the same things I was, and what we might call a higher cultural level," she said recently. "I didn't have to cope with that."

She did pretty well with what she had, though. Recently the world agreed and gave Alice Munro the Nobel Prize for Literature.

Take Two %#@ and Call Me in the Morning

*M*y doctor is a gem. A magnificent diamond. One of the crown jewels of the Canadian medical establishment. He is an insightful practitioner, a brilliant diagnostician, an inspired clinician and a tireless champion for anyone fortunate enough to count themselves among his patients. My doctor is smart, down to earth, empathetic and charismatic. In case you haven't guessed, I love the guy, but . . .

He writes like a three-year-old.

I'm not talking scrawly or crabbed or merely sloppy writing. I'm talking about penmanship so spectacularly horrendous it looks like it might be written in Aramaic. By an orangutan holding a ballpoint in his teeth. This is writing that ruptures the outer boundaries of cursive communication. A prescription from my doctor looks like a piece of paper that's been dive-bombed by a squadron of ink-soaked, methamphetamine-addled kamikaze fruit flies.

I know doctors should be forgiven their scrawls because they have to write a lot of things, and fast. Well, here's a flash: so do news reporters. The difference is reporters have to be able to read their own writing when it comes time to type it out.

Doctors have no such problem. That thankless chore falls to their receptionist or to some poor chump down in the pharmacy.

Of course it doesn't help that a lot of prescriptions employ a language that's been extinct for 2,000 years. Do doctors and pharmacists speak Latin? No, but they write and read it every day. Even the word for prescription—Rx—is a medieval English translation of the Latin original. It means "Receive thou."

Or in plain English—take.

The language of prescriptions written by English-speaking physicians borders on the Kafkaesque. In a sane universe the medical short form for "after meals" might be "AM," right? Wrong. It's "PC." For "twice daily" the secret code is "BID" whereas "QOD" is "every other day."

For some reason we've decided to cut doctors some slack about this. We treat their sloppy handwriting as a kind of amusing cultural cliché like thrifty Scotsmen, gesticulating Italians and snobby Brits.

Except it's not funny. According to a report in *Time* magazine, preventable medication mistakes injure 1.5 million American patients every year. It also claims that sloppy handwriting and/or improper deciphering of prescriptions kills 7,000 patients annually worldwide.

I'm not the only one that thinks this is lunacy. So does Louis Francescutti—Dr. Francescutti to the rest of us. He is president of the Royal College of Physicians and Surgeons and he's fed up with the prescriptive status quo. Two years ago Dr. Francescutti reviewed the case of Nova Scotia nurse Wilfred Douglas Gordon, one of the few medical practitioners to be officially reprimanded for his incomprehensible notations on nurses' notes and patients' charts. Dr. Francescutti told reporters, "It's totally unacceptable that we're still handwriting—that's how the monks did it. Everything should be dictated or typed."

I say Amen to that. I'd say a lot more but I've got a doctor's appointment this afternoon. Sure hope I see him before he sees this.

Part 9

AH, SALT SPRING!

And the Oscar Goes To . . .

You know the old joke. Question: Why does the Canadian cross the road? Answer: To get to the middle.

Well, new answer: To pick up the Oscar. The 85th edition of the Oscar awards ceremony took place a couple of years ago, but on Salt Spring it still feels like it happened last night. And why not? Considering that our governments have done all they can to shut down the film industry in this country, we came out of it not too shabbily. An Oscar for Toronto composer Mychael Danna for Best Original Score, *Life of Pi*; another Oscar for Vancouver-based Guillaume Rocheron for Best Visual Effects, *Life of Pi*. Which, let us not forget, is based on the Canadian book of the same name written by Canadian Yann Martel. And of course the Best Overall Film, *Argo*, is based on the saga of the Canadian heroes who bailed out their American Embassy colleagues in Iran.

Oh yeah, and one other Oscar. To Jim Erickson for Best Production Design on the film *Lincoln*.

That would be Jim Erickson . . . of Salt Spring Island. I wish I could say "my good pal and neighbour Jim Erickson" but in fact I've never met the guy. Or maybe I have and didn't know it. He seems to be a very self-effacing chap. He watched the Oscars not from the star-studded Dolby Theatre in Los Angeles but in the comfort of his own living room, here on Salt Spring Island.

Mind you, he dug out his mothballed tuxedo for the occasion.

Didn't he regret not being there, missing out on all the glamour and the sizzle, asked a CBC reporter? Not really, said Jim. He liked being at home with his family and a bowl of popcorn. "Besides," he said, "If I was there I'd have to fly home. And I WAS home."

Would he be heading back to Hollywood to capitalize on his Oscar win and make huge bucks for future projects? Mmmmm, nah, said Jim. He's retiring. He's more than earned his Hollywood bones, having been nominated for his work in *There Will Be Blood* some years ago. His other credits include *Watchmen*, *Water For Elephants* and *Ali*. "After *Lincoln*," Erickson said, "there's just not much else that I can think of that I want to do. I've had a really wonderful career, so why not go out on a high point instead of dribbling out toward the end?"

Excellent point. There were a lot of memorable moments in the 85th annual Oscar Awards. Daniel Day-Lewis's speech, Seth MacFarlane's one-liners, First Lady Michele Obama naming *Argo* best picture, and producer Ben Affleck thanking Canada for making the movie possible.

But my favourite moment is an imagined one. I'm imagining Jim Erickson sitting in his Salt Spring living room, spilling popcorn on the lapels of his tuxedo as his name is announced to millions and millions of people around the world.

Let's Make a Deal, Salt Spring Style

I have a confession to make: I never watch *Dragons' Den*. That's because I HAVE watched Kevin O'Leary being interviewed and he's the kind of guy I instinctively cover my groin and throat and back away from at cocktail parties. O'Leary's a shark. I've got nothing against sharks; I just prefer to do my dog-paddling elsewhere.

That said, I had to break my embargo, dive in and watch the show when Island resident Palu Rainbowsong was featured on an episode. I wouldn't have missed that for all the tiger sharks in the South China Sea.

Palu Rainbowsong? You don't know Palu Rainbowsong? Hey, he's Salt Spring Island's most recognized natural resource. Palu is to Salt Spring like maple syrup is to Quebec; like potatoes are to PEI; like bitumen is to Fort McMurray. He's short, stocky, with a flyaway reddish-grey beard. He wears a toque and various vaguely East Indian robes. He looks like an extra left over from one of the crowd scenes in *Lord of the Rings*. And, in a Hobbity kind of way, he's friendly, greeting many of our tourists as they make their way ashore from the ferry.

Okay, it's not JUST about being friendly. Palu's trying to sell you something. It's an out-of-body experience. Palu manufactures what he calls the Solar Meditation Bow. It sort of looks like an archery-type bow except it's made out of a piece of PVC pipe and there are feathers and bangly stuff hanging from the bowstring. Palu encourages would-be customers to look toward the sun. Then he holds the Solar Meditation Bow up between the sun and the person's eyes, gives it a twang and encourages the would-be customer to, I don't know, enter another dimension, I suppose.

Hey. It's Salt Spring.

Does the Solar Meditation Bow work? Well, I tried it and all I got was a mild headache, but as any of my teachers and a couple of ex-partners would attest I'm not a very enlightened guy.

Point is, and I'm not making this up, Palu Rainbowsong was flown to Toronto to tape an appearance on *Dragons' Den*, during which he tried to convince Kevin O'Leary and his fellow meat eaters to finance the production of Solar Meditation Bows for a national—even international—marketplace.

Was he successful? Not even close. But wouldn't it have been great to see Kevin O'Leary stare into a Solar Meditation Bow and murmur, "Yeah, Mr. Rainbowsong, I think this thing's got legs."

Sheepwrecked on Salt Spring

I 've never met the British environmental writer George Monbiot but if I ever do we'll have lots to talk about. Sheep, for instance. I come from Salt Spring Island, which doesn't have an official T-shirt or a crest but if it did you can be sure there'd be a sheep on it. Sheep epitomize the island. They're everywhere. And what a great mascot! What's more loveable than a cute and cuddly, white and fluffy, bleating and baaing sheep?

Well . . . depends on the company you keep. George Monbiot, for instance. In his latest book, *Feral*, there's a chapter entitled "Sheepwrecked" (you can tell where this is going, can't you?). Monbiot writes and I quote: "I have an unhealthy obsession with sheep. I hate them."

Contrary to the "sheep-may-safely-graze," Disneyesque image that sheep enjoy in other circles, Monbiot calls them "a white plague. A slow-burning ecological disaster which has done more damage to the living systems of Great Britain than either climate change or industrial pollution."

Harsh words from George. His contention is that when it comes to sheep, for the past three or four centuries we've had the wool pulled over our eyes. While poets wrote respectful odes and musicians sang heartwarming songs about the little lambs of God, the greedy little herbivores were scarifying the English landscape by nibbling and grazing the uplands right down to bald earth. Thing is, British sheep are allowed to graze in the national parks so they've had a transformative influence there as well.

Monbiot's solution: bring back the wolves. I've a hunch that might not fly in England's green and pleasant land. In any case I'm happy to report that it hasn't come to that on Salt Spring. We still love our sheep here. Perhaps because we're more, um, practical than your average poet or troubadour. When it comes to sheep and especially to lambs, Salt Springers are closer to Sir Walter Scott's wife than we are to Sir Walter. The story goes that one day Sir Walter and Lady Scott were out for a stroll and came to a pasture wherein a number of ewes and lambs frolicked and gambolled as ewes and lambs are wont to do.

"Ah, 'tis no wonder," intoned Sir Walter, "that poets from the earliest ages, have made the lamb the emblem of peace and innocence."

"Delightful animals, indeed," said Lady Scott. "Especially with mint sauce."

When it comes to understanding our fellow critters it's always a matter of perspective. My dad used to deal in sheep and lambs. We kept a few on the farm. I remember as a teenager taking a walk with a new date. Much like Sir Walter and Lady Scott, we too came upon some sheep. No lambs, though. Just a ram and a ewe and the ram was . . . doing what rams frequently do with ewes, if you catch my drift.

I was a bashful teenager but I knew an opening when I saw one. I turned to my date and said, "That looks like fun. I wouldn't mind doing what that ram is doing."

My date shrugged and said, "Well, it's your ewe."

Waiting for the Big One

There's a special something that comes with living on the West Coast. Well, there are a lot of special somethings but there's one big one. I call it the Damoclean Factor. You know Damocles? Greek guy of legend who was allowed to sit on the king's throne only as long as he could stand sitting under a huge sword over his head that was held up by a single hair from a horse's mane. Damocles caved in pretty quick and begged to go back to his life as a commoner.

Living on the West Coast is a bit like living under that Damoclean sword except that our threat isn't from something hanging over us. Our threat comes from below. Earthquake. We all know we're overdue for a biggie. The Big Ones come along about every 400 years on average and our last big one hit in January of 1700, so we're definitely in the twilight zone.

And of course for those of us who live on islands, there's a one-two punch that awaits. It's not just the earthquake, is it? I remember years ago when I told one hard-core Torontonian why I was leaving that infested, congested, polluted rat race for a more bucolic life on the West Coast, he grunted, "Where you going?" Salt Spring Island, I told him. "I have one word for you," he smirked. "It's a Japanese word: tsunami."

Well, point taken. Except it turns out he was wrong. For my island anyway, as well as for most of the populated centres on Vancouver Island and the Strait of Georgia.

The Capital Regional District has released a report that says any major earthquake will most likely originate along what they call the Cascadia subduction zone, which runs 80 or 90 kilometers off the seaward side of Vancouver Island. Which means the relatively uninhabited west coast of Vancouver Island will see substantial tsunami damage, but those of us hunkered on the leeward, Salish Sea side will be protected. The wave action will be greatly slowed down by the Strait of Juan de Fuca, like pouring a gallon of milk into a narrow funnel.

Mind you, we won't be protected from the earthquake. But what the heck, we're Canadians, eh? We'll handle it like the Prairie folks do when somebody from Toronto shakes their head in wonder on hearing the temperature in Saskatoon, say, has hit 40 below. "Jeez," the Toronto guy will say. "How can you stand it that cold?"

Well, the Prairie people say, it's a dry cold.

That's the way we'll handle the Big One on Salt Spring. Yes, we'll say. It's a catastrophe, but it's a dry catastrophe.

Who Did You Use to Be?

You meet the strangest usetabes on Salt Spring Island. See that guy outside the gelato place? Used to be a regular on *The Rockford Files* with James Garner. See the lady in the peasant skirt wearing a boiled felt fedora? Used to be the Paris correspondent for *Newsweek* magazine. See the guy taking photos of the boats in the harbour? Used to be a roadie for the Grateful Dead.

See the quiet guy at the end of the bar? The big fella with the ham-hock hands and the lived-in face, nursing a cup of tea? Nobody knows who he used to be and he isn't telling. But every once in a while he drops a hint.

Like the time we were all sitting around talking about the drug dealers in Centennial Park. We have (surprise, surprise) drugs on Salt Spring. Including the nasty ones—meth, coke, crack, heroin, OxyContin. And the park in the middle of Ganges appears to be the marketplace of choice. The Mounties watch it pretty closely but it's a fair-sized park with lots of nooks and crannies. We were talking about how brazen the drug dealers were getting when we heard a little laugh from the big guy at the end of the bar. Without looking up from his teacup, he started to talk.

"We had two guys dealing drugs to school kids in Prince

George," he said softly. "Right outside the high school. In a Mercury Marauder.

"The teachers phoned the cops and they came to investigate but as soon as the cruiser left the Merc was back in front of the school. This went on for most of a week. Then a friend and I decided enough was enough. We got in my truck, roared up and cut off the car so they couldn't get away, grabbed the two guys—they were forty, forty-five maybe. We duct-taped their wrists behind them and threw them in their own back seat. Then we took 'em—my buddy drove the Merc, I drove my truck—to a shack way at the end of a logging road outside PG. We didn't beat them up or anything. We just talked to them. Then we took their clothes and left them there. It was June so it wasn't cold. But there were a lot of bugs. And we also reminded them it was bear country. Then my pal and I drove away. We took the truck and the Merc Marauder.

"They had a thirty-two-mile walk back to town. In their underwear."

He sipped his tea. "I don't know what happened to them," he said. "They never showed up around the high school again. But they were a nasty pair. We opened the trunk of the Marauder and found a sawed-off shotgun and a canvas satchel. There was two hundred and sixty-six thousand bucks in it."

He took another sip of tea. We waited. Finally somebody said, "What did you do with the money?"

He looked at us like we were perhaps a little slow. "Turned it into the cops," he said. "It was drug money."

So that's pretty much all we know about who the big guy at the end of the bar used to be. We know that he spends some time in Prince George. And we know that if you're dealing, you'd better hope the Mounties bust you before he does.

Happy Trails, Tex

Salt Spring doesn't have a Hitchhiker's Hall of Fame but if it did, the guy standing closest to the road with his thumb out would be Barney Peter Holmes. He was never hard to spot if you were looking to give somebody a ride. Or even if you weren't. The man looked like Santa with a hangover. White beard, scowly face, backpack, a walking staff. Oh, and a big crumpled 10-gallon Stetson hat on his head. Which is why everybody called him Tex.

Except not to his face. Tex, I mean Barney, for some reason took a dislike to being called Tex after 10 or 20 or 30 years of answering to it. Took off the Stetson and replaced it with a ball cap. "Don't call me Tex," he'd growl.

Tex hitchhiked everywhere. Legend had it that he hitchhiked to the Calgary Stampede every year and never missed the Luxton Rodeo near Victoria. Even made it to Nova Scotia at least once. But mostly he just hitchhiked into town and back from his house deep in the south end of the island. Did that pretty much every day. A remarkable feat considering that rides on Salt Spring are somewhat limited and if you gave Tex a ride once you wouldn't necessarily be in a rush to pick him up again.

He could be . . . cantankerous. He was certainly opinionated. And he was a strong believer in the Farley Mowat principle of never letting the truth get in the way of a good story. He grumbled about his troubles as the owner of a large ranch, the number of horses he ran and the hundreds of head of cattle he owned, not to mention the unreliable hired hands who gave him grief.

There's an old western expression among ranchers about somebody being "all hat and no cattle." Tex had the hat. And as his niece so kindly put it, "To him, the ranch was real."

Tex was challenged. And he was challenging. I confess that I usually found a reason or two not to pick him up on my trips into and out of town. I wasn't going very far, I had the dog in the back seat, the car was full of groceries. Or just it was Tex and I didn't have the strength. I rationalized that somebody else would be sure to give him a ride.

Well, I don't have to wrestle with the guilt anymore. I no longer have the option of offering the island institution a ride. Barney Peter Holmes passed on at the age of 82.

My loss. Salt Spring's too. We need all the characters we can get. Happy trails . . . Barney.

Intruders—Buck Naked!

I'm not sure how you feel about the problem of homeless indigents carousing and sleeping rough in our parks and green spaces but I've got an open field in front of my place. An old apple orchard in fact. And when I opened my gate the other day I counted 13 of them—13! Milling around, buck naked, scratching and relieving themselves, snoozing and schmoozing. I tell ya, I'm as easygoing as the next Canuck but I'm getting ticked off.

That's ticked as in deer ticked. The orchard ne'er-do-wells I'm talking about all belong to the same tribe—*Odocoileus hemionus columbianus*, to wit. Which is to say blacktail deer. The Gulf Islands in general and my island in particular have an overabundance of blacktails and they've worn out their welcome.

Okay, that's not quite fair. The blacktails were here long before we white faces showed up. But then so were cougars, coyotes and bears, all of which enjoyed hearty diets that prominently featured venison. Unwisely, we wiped out the cougar, coyote and bear populations, which was like handing a group Get Out of Jail Free card to the blacktails, who immediately went forth and multiplied.

Big time.

It's pretty difficult to tell how many deer are on Salt Spring but unofficial surveys range from "plenty" to "way too many."

What's more they aren't exactly shy and reclusive. You can see deer along roadsides, in parks, even downtown from time to time, and anytime at all in gardens or yards that aren't fenced. It's not good for the island ecosystem. Heck, it's not even good for the deer.

Of those 13 deer I saw across the road at least four were recently born fawns, scrawny and patchy looking. They won't be getting any fatter in the next three or four months. My guess is they're about one snowstorm away from a miserable demise. But they'll do sufficient damage before they go. Peter Arcese, a conservation biologist with the University of British Columbia, has been studying the Gulf Island ecosystem for more than 30 years. He affirms that the blacktail appetite threatens the natural vegetation and that the variety of plants and shrubs are shrivelling.

What to do? Well, we could round 'em up and ship them off somewhere, I suppose. Good luck. Deer do travel in herds but they don't respond well to border collies, merge signs or men with clipboards and lassoes.

Or we could sterilize them, but that's pretty tricky and hideously expensive and not guaranteed to work.

Failing that I suppose we could (cough, cough) cull them.

What? WHAT? Did someone utter the C word?

On Salt Spring? Well, some do mention the possibility of a deer cull from time to time and they always use the word "cull" rather than "kill" because "cull" is so much more delicate. It sounds so inoffensive. Somewhere between weeding the garden and clipping your toenails. Unless you're a deer.

Contrary to popular belief it is legal to hunt deer on Salt Spring, but just barely. First you have to get a special permit to even discharge a gun. Then you have to get a hunting licence. Then you have to restrict yourself to hunting where there are no residences (good luck with that, too). If you belly wriggle your way through all those hoops you are allowed to shoot two bucks per year but only bucks with antlers. Oh, and the season runs from September 10 to December 10. All in all not a pastime calculated to put much of a dent in the deer population.

Speaking of dents, that's another consideration you need to

take into account if you're travelling around the island, particularly in the fall. The Salt Spring RCMP detachment issued a press release that reads: "Police are asking motorists to be extra alert at this time of year. Fall is mating season for the local deer population and their thoughts are on romance, not vehicle avoidance."

It's true. Salt Spring deer—never Rhodes scholars at the best of times—are particularly loopy and unpredictable in the fall. Aggressive too. A couple of years ago a randy buck actually charged a guy on a motor scooter and knocked him off. He ended up in the Lady Minto Hospital (the guy, not the deer).

I'm working on a road sign that I plan to erect for unwary tourists driving off the ferry at Fulford Harbour. It'll read: CAUTION: HORNY DEER. AND WE DON'T MEAN ANTLERS.

Salt Spring: The Plane Truth

*T*he folk singer Valdy famously described Salt Spring as "a difference of opinion surrounded by water." The fanciful wit of the first part of that observation can obscure the flat reality of the second: we are surrounded by water. It separates Salt Spring from the other Gulf Islands, from Vancouver Island on the west and from the looming hulk of North America on the east. It is our Pyrenees, our English Channel, our demilitarized zone, our medieval castle moat. That water must be negotiated and overcome by any who would visit us.

There are options for those who would. You can swim, paddleboard, sail a boat or take a BC ferry—all of which are somewhat tiresome and demanding in one way or another. Time consuming, too. I've never tried the dog-paddle or the paddleboard but even with luck, either option would set you back the best part of a sunny windless day. As for the ferry, well I used to commute once a week from Salt Spring to Vancouver. The one-way trip including bus transfer was six hours, door to door.

But there's another way to get from there to here. You can take the magic carpet. It will wisk you from downtown Vancouver to downtown Ganges in less than half an hour. The magic carpet you will ride will probably be a de Havilland Beaver, that sturdy quarter horse of a seaplane that's been working the Canadian skies since the middle of the last century. There are three airlines that service Salt Spring with more than half a dozen daily flights: Harbour Air, Seair and my favourite, Salt Spring Air. Altogether they offer more than half a dozen flights daily, but forget the cattle chute shuffle and in-flight crush of standard commercial flights. On your flight to Salt Spring you will share your plane with no more than five other passengers—two in the back, three in the middle seat, one up by the pilot.

Oh, and unlike some national airlines I could name, your luggage, up to 25 pounds, flies free of charge.

The cost? Less than you'd pay to take your spouse, a couple of kids and your station wagon on the ferry from Tsawwassen. Plus you'll fly only a few hundred feet over the water, giving you an eagle's-eye view of Stanley Park, Vancouver harbour, a couple of Gulf Islands and, if you're extremely lucky, a flurry of porpoises or even a pod of orcas plying the Georgia Strait.

And as I said, it's fast and direct. One minute you're standing at the counter in downtown Vancouver; less than half an hour later you're sipping a cappuccino at the Tree House cafe in Ganges.

So, which one to choose? Seair, Harbour or Salt Spring Air? I've flown them all and they all offer excellent service. But as I said earlier, my personal favourite is Salt Spring Air, for sentimental reasons.

Years ago, back when I was a Salt Spring newbie, I boarded a Beaver for my first flight from Ganges to Vancouver. I was the lone passenger. The pilot, an island character named St. Clair McColl who would go on to become a co-owner of Salt Spring Air, turned to me, grandly proffering a greasy paper bag and inquired, "Croissant?"

You just don't get that kind of attention on Air Canada.

A Different Kind of Library

I've talked before about Salt Spring Island's shiny new library. (Well, almost new. It opened its doors in 2013.)

It's a beauty—all wood and glass, located in the heart of downtown Ganges. It's already established itself as a popular oasis for islanders but it has plenty of competition here on Salt Spring.

I'm thinking of one of my favourite island libraries located right beside a 120-year-old church called Saint Mary's, a lanky, brown-shingle-clad edifice about half a mile on from the Fulford Harbour ferry terminal. This is a church that was founded in family tragedy. Back in 1889 the son of a farmer named John Sparrow was accidentally shot and killed by some good old boys who were pit-lamping deer. In his grief, John Sparrow dedicated several acres of land as a site for a new church. Volunteers pitched in with lumber, some surplus pews were donated by congregations in Victoria and in 1894 St. Mary's church was consecrated and open for business. Which brings me to the library I mentioned earlier. It's open air, free admission and covers at least a half an acre around St. Mary's.

It's a graveyard. St. Mary's church is garlanded with gravestones and markers both fancy and not so.

As befits a century-old institution, there are plenty of your standard funereal memorials— everything from plain crosses to ornate marble slabs—but this being Salt Spring there's a spattering of markers that tend toward the non-traditional.

Rose Donnelly, 1920–1988, for instance. In addition to a tombstone, Rose's resting place is covered with trophies—tennis, darts and bowling trophies—all a-jumble.

That tells you more about Rose than a conventional epitaph ever could.

Then there's Jan Bertram von Stolk. His marker informs us that he was born in Rotterdam in 1925, died on Salt Spring in 2002. His grave is marked not with a cross but an oval.

He left a message, too. Not the usual Rest In Peace, or Asleep in the Arms of the Lord but this, chiselled into stone: "Between Wish and Action is the Decision to Connect."

Hm. Makes you think.

And then there's Daniel Snook. Daniel died at the age of only 20. His grave is decorated with a beautiful, ever-so-slightly sculpted boulder the size of the prize-winning pumpkin at the fall fair. It's surrounded by a scattering of smaller stones, a favourite fishing lure and a heartbreakingly beautiful laminated photo of a young smiling man taken from us long before his time.

Graveyards are fascinating libraries. Their stones are full of facts and wishes, some profound, some facetious. In an Edinburgh churchyard there is a tombstone over the mortal remains of a Scottish dentist named Brown. Its inscription reads: "Stranger, tread this ground with gravity. Dentist Brown is filling his last cavity."

The American philosopher Ben Franklin took longer to make his last observation. His tombstone reads: "The body of Benjamin Franklin, Printer, like the covers of an old book, its contents torn out . . . lies food for worms. Yet the work itself shall not be lost, for it will (as he believed) appear once more in a new and more beautiful edition, corrected and amended by the author."

Now that is both profound and witty. But for pure pithy epitaphery (if there is such a word) I prefer the inscription that adorns the simple grave of a Salt Springer named Steve Asproloupos that I came across in the St. Mary's churchyard. It doesn't give a lot of biographical detail about Mr. Asproloupos. He was born in 1937, died in 2002. But I like to think you can imagine a lot about the man from the two-word inscription chiselled below those dates.

It reads: "Gone fishing."

A Change of Life

So. What've you got planned for the next three years of your life?

Wait—let me fine-tune that. What are you doing for the next three years, three months, three weeks, three days, three hours and three minutes of your life?

If you're like me you can perhaps come up with the vague outline of an answer to that question. Barring a lottery windfall or a major earthquake it'll be a lot of same old same old, with a few unforecastable hills and dales and blind curves tossed in. We like to think we're in charge of our lives but we're really just wood chips in a stream, carried by currents and eddies over waterfalls, past deadheads and sandbars we can seldom see or control.

Not like a friend of mine here on Salt Spring. She knows exactly what she'll be doing for the next three years, three months, three weeks, three days, three hours and three minutes. Or rather, what she won't be doing. She won't be driving a car, or going to a movie or shopping in a mall. She won't be watching TV, or listening to a radio or answering a phone. She won't have a phone. And she won't be on Salt Spring, or even in Canada. She'll be in a small cabin in the bush in rural Washington state.

She'll be at a Buddhist retreat.

It ain't a holiday. For starters she'll be getting up at 3 a.m. (there's that number three again) every morning for silent meditation. That will be followed by a silent breakfast, then more meditation, then chores, all done in silence. She will get to speak with her fellow retreaters three times a day for 30-minute intervals. More threes.

Well, three is a number that's sacred not just to Buddhists. The ancient Greeks had the Three Graces; Christianity has the Holy Trinity; the Torah calls three the number of truth. Even our fairy tales feature threes: the Three Little Pigs, Goldilocks and the Three Bears. Macbeth had the Three Witches. Our whole planetary existence is a three-act play: past, present, future.

My friend has closed the door to her past. She's selling her house on Salt Spring. She's getting rid of her car. She's gifted her two beloved dogs to friends. Her future—the next three years, months, weeks, days, hours and minutes of it at any rate—she will live in the present. In a small cabin in the Washington woods. Without the distractions of what we are pleased to call "normal" life.

Won't she be terribly lonely? Well, loneliness is an attitude. The writer Paul Tillich said: "We have the word loneliness to express the pain of being alone; we have the word 'solitude' to express the glory of being alone."

Another fellow who spent a fair bit of time in a cabin in the woods, Henry David Thoreau, wrote: "I have never found a companion that was so companionable as solitude."

And good old Rumi, the thirteenth-century Persian mystic declared: "A little while alone in your room will prove more valuable than anything else that can ever be given you."

You can say that again. And again. (Three times lucky.)

Good luck, Maggie.

Salt Spring's Lunar Eclipse

*A*h, September. This is the beginning of the bittersweet season on Salt Spring. It is the season of departures. The longest, sunniest, driest summer in my memory has now departed, symbolically at least. Hummingbirds, those Jack Russells of the bird world, are tanking up at my feeders in preparation for their trip south. The Canada geese are . . . can Canada geese grouse? Well, they're grumbling for sure. Beeping and honking in the bay as they jostle for position to, very soon, depart the island, flying in regulation V formations.

Most glorious and resonant of all, the biggest, most unruly, largely unpredictable summer flock on the island has finally departed for another year.

I refer, of course, to tourists.

I know. It ill-behooves a Salt Spring Islander to moan about the tourists, I realize that. They come each summer in their Oakley sunglasses and Tilley shorts and they leave behind much more attractive deposits than, say, the Canada geese do. Tourists leave money. They fuel the island B&Bs, the restaurants, the Saturday market vendors, all and sundry island shopkeepers and service providers, I give you that.

But my, they—how do I say this diplomatically? They do alter the island dynamic.

Our one town of Ganges, for instance, is pretty much from Canada Day to Labour Day snarled in one massive Gordian knot of cars, buses and slow-moving rafts of perambulating tourists. Salt Spring has plenty of side streets but it has only one main thoroughfare and it runs right through the middle of town. Well, in summer, "runs" is not quite the right verb. Because tourists, bless their lollygagging hearts, don't seem to realize that it IS a road. They think it's a midway, or a gigantic outdoor mall. They drift across the road in clumps and clots, not looking left or right, stopping in the middle to consult their Chamber of Commerce maps or to take selfies in front of the picturesque fire hall.

Meanwhile, islanders, intent on getting to the dentist up in the hill, or Mouat's hardware down by the dock, sit in their becalmed vehicles, idling and percolating.

Waiting and praying. For September.

And now it's here. And if you listen closely you can hear a massive, island-wide sigh of relief. We have the island back. At least until spring.

Old-timers tell me that years ago there was a tradition on Salt Spring. They say that in the old days when the last BC Ferry sailed from Long Harbour on the Labour Day Monday carrying the last load of tourists from our island, a rag-tag line of islanders would string out along the shore to send the tourists off with cheery waves and huzzahs. And then, just as the ferry steamed by these islanders would turn their backs as one, bend at the waist and . . . drop their drawers.

Just another island legend I'm sure. But still, you haven't really lived until you've seen the moon(s) from Salt Spring Island.